# Monkseaton Village
## Volume One

## by Charlie Steel

*Best Wishes.*

*The Black Horse Inn, 1937.*

*Previous page: The Dunn family were a well known and respected family in the Monkseaton area. Their horses and farm vehicles were often entered in local agricultural shows and frequently won prizes and awards. In this 1905 photograph, one of their immaculately liveried carts driven by John (Jack) Dunn stands near the Black Horse Inn (next to Coronation Row), Monkseaton loaded with milk churns. The identity of the young boy is unknown.*

# Summerhill Books

Summerhill Books publishes local history books on Northumberland, Durham and Tyneside. To receive a catalogue of our titles send a stamped addressed envelope to:

Andrew Clark, Summerhill Books, PO Box 1210, Newcastle-upon-Tyne NE99 4AH

or email: summerhillbooks@yahoo.co.uk

or visit our website to view our full range of books: **www.summerhillbooks.co.uk**

Copyright Charlie Steel 2012

First published in 2012 by

Summerhill Books
PO Box 1210, Newcastle-upon-Tyne NE99 4AH

www.summerhillbooks.co.uk

email: summerhillbooks@yahoo.co.uk

ISBN: 978-1-906721-49-7

# CONTENTS

# PREFACE

I believe that any local history publication should begin with an apology, and this book is no exception. The apology is based on the fact that no-one can guarantee the reliability or accuracy of the information, because the information is only as accurate as the source from which it was obtained.

Local history research can be quite complex, and involves seeking out many different sources to procure the required information, however drawbacks become apparent whenever a conflict of information is encountered. For example, it is common to find many variations in the spelling of words, names and places etc. and likewise dates can also conflict unless original copies of the relevant documentation are available to make them indisputable. Even full paragraphs and articles from old books or documents can be confusing and occasionally misleading, depending on how they are studied. Sometimes it requires logical interpretation and perhaps some calculated judgement to process and simplify that information to make it easily understood.

With this in mind, I have researched the information in this publication to the best of my ability, and attempted to ensure its accuracy as far as possible, however I am well aware that there will always be some details which are open to debate, especially those which may not be documented, or are taken from the personal recollections of the contributors.

If any obvious inaccuracies are found, it would be advantageous to advise me along with a provable reference source rather than being critical of the content, and this way with your help, they can be corrected for the benefit of any future editions.

*Charlie Steel*
*May 2012*

# INTRODUCTION

*'What you need to know about the past is that no matter what has happened, it has all worked together to bring you to this very moment. And this is the moment you can choose to make everything new. Right now.'* – Unknown Author.

The study of local history evokes great interest and curiosity to many people. In my view, the past and present are inseparable, because what we have today has been formed by past events. The study of the past therefore illuminates the present. Astronomer and Scientist, Dr Carl Sagan is quoted as saying; *'You have to know the past to understand the present'*, and this is perfectly true. Light hearted clichés suggest that *'History is a thing of the past'*, and *'Nostalgia isn't what it used to be'*.

Whichever way you look at it, and whether you like it or loathe it, local history is a significant part of our heritage. It can conjure up colourful visions of days gone by, evoking memories of the past and allowing us an opportunity to reflect on our background. For example, there will surely be many occasions when someone has been shown an old picture or photograph and thought: *'I can remember that'*, and soon the image has inspired a topic for conversation or debate. That was perhaps the case some years ago when I inherited a number of local photographs which I began to study and research. As a result, I decided to compile a book, which was published in 2000 and entitled; *Monkseaton and Hillheads*. The book was simply a basic pictorial overview of the two areas in times gone by; however in those days, the publishers dictated the terms by imposing control of the layout, the content and the number of pages, which resulted in lots of information having to be omitted. Nevertheless, the book still proved very popular. Strictly speaking, the book is not exactly 'out of date', but as time marched on, I felt that the time had come to consider another look at the history of Monkseaton from a different perspective and extend the available information. This book is the result and is the first of two volumes which has taken over 10 years to research and compile, presenting a more comprehensive and in depth history of the village and its people. It also contains a renewed selection of pictures, photographs, maps and images, many of which have never been published before. The information it contains should prove to be a popular source of reference for years to come. I hope you enjoy reading it.

*Charlie Steel*
*Monkseaton, May 2012*

*Staff of the Auxiliary Fire Service, based at Wilson's Garage during the Second World War.*

4

# ACKNOWLEDGEMENTS & CONTRIBUTORS

It is not possible to put a book together of this nature without the assistance of many other people. Over a number of years, the people listed below have each made a significant contribution to the content of this publication, and it is therefore important that they are personally acknowledged by name:

| ITEM | CONTRIBUTOR |
| --- | --- |
| Coronation Row | Nigel Monckton-Milnes |
| Deakin Printers | Graeme Thorndyke |
| Ewen's Butchers | John Ewen |
| Foxhunters Trading Estate | Bill Bush |
| Frankland Mount | Andrew & Helen Keenan and Beryl Merrit |
| Gofton's | Irene Gofton |
| Jenkinson Glaziers | Florence Taggart and Steve Bradley |
| MacGregor's | Rob Miller |
| Maps | Ordnance Survey |
| Monkseaton Brewery | Mike Sowter |
| Monkseaton Garage | Tom Shields |
| Newsteads Farm | Harry Edwards |
| Norie Electrical | Reg Norie |
| Outram's Garage | Dave Wilson |
| Red House Farm | John Dunn, Moya Sharp and Robert Preston North Tyneside Council |
| Reeves Timber & Hardware Shop | Colin Reeves |
| St Ronan's Road | Peter Hasselby |
| Souter Park | Bill Davison |
| Street Development | Ian Sutherland |
| Ship Inn | Fred & Joyce Turnbull |
| Taylor's Garage | Jack Taylor, John Taylor and Christine Morton |
| Tyne Taxis | Doug Boyd |
| West Monkseaton Open Cast | Keith Haddock and Tom Tait |
| Wilson's Garage | Geoff Stewart, Tony Craven and Nigel Tait |

Special thanks also go to all the staff of North Tyneside Local Studies Library, especially Diane Leggett and Alan Hildrew for their patience and valued assistance, and Andrew Clark for his valuable help, advice and support.

# SOURCES OF REFERENCE

Many reference sources and publications have also been utilised in order to complete this publication, however some of the more significant ones include the following:

Ordnance Survey Mapping

North Shields Library – Local Studies Centre

| | |
| --- | --- |
| Remembering the Past – Resourcing the Future | Kath Smith and all relevant contributors to the North Shields Library Club |
| Historical Notes on Cullercoats, Whitley and Monkseaton | William Weaver Tomlinson |
| Wards Directories | R. Ward & Sons |
| Monkseaton Conservation Area Character Appraisal | North Tyneside Council |
| Wikipedia | Internet Based |

# HISTORICAL OVERVIEW

**WHITLEY** was first mentioned about the year 1100 when King Henry I conferred it with other possessions on the Priory of Tynemouth and it was referred to in ancient documents and maps before that date as Witelei, Wyteley, Hwyteleg, Witelithe, Wheteley, Wytheleye, Whitlaw, Whitlathe and Whitlag. Whitley is also referred to in the charters of King Henry II, King Richard I and King John, confirming to the priors their possessions and liberties.

Whitley was connected with the Crusades when Pope Nicholas IV granted to Edward I the first-fruits and tenths of all ecclesiastical possessions for six years to defray the expenses of an expedition to the Holy Land. A valuation was made of the spiritual and temporal goods of the Priory on 26th March 1292, when the yearly rents from Whitley were returned as 20 shillings, and the tithes as 9 marks.

About the beginning of the 14th century, the manor of Whitley was held from the Prior of Tynemouth by a singular feudal service called the Conveyes which seems to have originated from John de Whitley. Richard de Emeldon, eighteen times Mayor of Newcastle and seven times its representative in Parliament, was the Lord of the Manor of Whitley in 1333.

On 9th April 1345, Edward III granted to Gilbert de Whitley a licence to crenellate his manor house at Whitley. To crenallate a house was to place battlements upon it. Before this could be done, the sanction of the Crown was often sought. Although the battlements were largely symbolic, this practice is an indication of the degree of insecurity felt even this far south during the Edwardian wars with Scotland. The licence and crenellations were a display of status. Only 2% of the small tower houses of the sort Gilbert built had licences. The 'sanction' of the crown was a sought-after bonus, but not a requirement.

After the Dissolution of the Monasteries, Whitley was held under the Crown for a time. By a grant of Edward VI dated 8th December 1551, it came into the hands of Dudley, Earl of Warwick who was created Duke of Northumberland. It remained in the Percy family until 1632 after which time the area appeared to be let at a yearly rental to various holders until it came into the possession of the Duke of Somerset on his marriage in 1682 with Elizabeth, the heiress of Joscelyn, the 11th Earl of Northumberland.

Whitley subsequently passed by inheritance to her granddaughter Elizabeth Seymour who had married Sir Hugh Smithson, a Yorkshire baronet, afterwards created Duke of Northumberland. Whitley has since been retained by descendants and the present Duke of Northumberland is the Lord of the Manor and principal landowner.

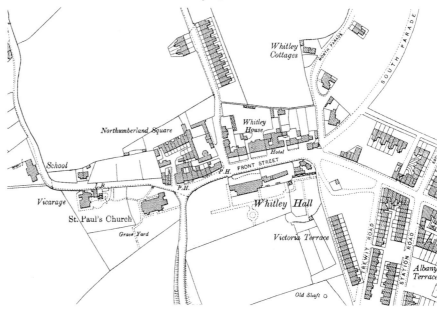

1873 saw an event of importance in the town's history by the establishment of the Whitley and Monkseaton Local Board. The district of the Local Board became the Urban District of Whitley and Monkseaton. There was however always a distinct cleavage between the two villages of Whitley and Monkseaton as the residents lived entirely separate lives, and this division even existed well into the 1900s. For example, in 1898, when Councillor John Appleby of West Farm, Monkseaton was made Vice Chairman of the Whitley and Monkseaton Urban District Council, the residents of Whitley were angry that a person who lived as far away as Monkseaton could not hope to understand the needs of the people of Whitley. Conversely, when the council borrowed £1,700 to lay out the first quarter mile of Promenade between Cullercoats and Percy Road, the residents of Monkseaton were vociferous in their objections at making a financial contribution towards the cost of something that most would never use or even see during their lifetime.

From the late 19th century and into the 20th century the adverse effects of the decline of local coalmining and dependent industries in the area were ameliorated by the emergence of Whitley as a seaside holiday resort. Its popularity with holidaymakers was helped by the opening of the North Tyne Loop railway line in 1882, connecting the coastal villages to Newcastle. The line followed the route of the present Metro line, and necessitated the building of a new railway station in the centre of the town, as well as another at Monkseaton. Both stations are still in use as Metro stations.

ARMORIAL BEARINGS
OF THE
BOROUGH OF WHITLEY BAY.
Granted by Letters Patent dated 23rd April, 1954.

NON·SIBI·SED·OMNIBUS

The town was known as Whitley until the 1890s, by which time the confusion of the name with Whitby, in Yorkshire, was often causing mail to be misdirected. The final straw came when an ex-resident died in Edinburgh and his body was to be buried in St Paul's churchyard, Whitley. Unfortunately, the body was transported to Whitby by mistake causing the funeral to be delayed. The council asked residents for suggestions for a new name, and the most popular choice was Whitley Bay. It has since been known as Whitley Bay, but many residents still refer to the town as 'Whitley'.

On the 1st January 1944 the Whitley and Monkseaton Urban District became the Whitley Bay Urban District and on 5th March 1954 it was granted its Royal Charter of Incorporation as the Borough of Whitley Bay. The charter was presented by HRH the Princess Royal at a ceremony in the town held on 14th April 1954. The Whitley Bay Parish Church is St Paul's Church which was provided by the Duke of Northumberland when the old parish of Tynemouth was divided in 1860. It was consecrated in 1864. The Local Government Act 1972 abolished the borough, with Hartley in the north of the borough going to Blyth Valley district in Northumberland, and the main part including Whitley and Monkseaton forming part of the Metropolitan Borough of North Tyneside in the Tyne and Wear area.

**MONKSEATON** is situated less than half a mile to the west of Whitley Bay, and its industries were common with that town, being chiefly coalmining and limestone quarrying. Wellfield and Earsdon stand to the north of the village, and here the landscape gradually changes into green belt as it extends into south east Northumberland. The earliest recorded evidence of human activity at Monkseaton is a rectilinear enclosure probably dating from the late Iron Age. Aerial photographs of the site show internal features including partitions and a roundhouse, with an entrance on the north east side and an old field boundary in the same area. A Roman terracotta lamp was also found in the area; however there is no indication of Roman occupation.

The first documentary references to Monkseaton medieval village date from the early 12th century (c.1106-16) when Henry I granted its lands to Tynemouth Priory. In 1295, it is known that Tynemouth Monastery's demesne in Monkseaton measured and contained 880 acres under cultivation and 173 acres of common land, waste, roads and buildings.

Study of antiquarian maps would suggest that the medieval boundaries have been preserved in the layout of the later village. At this time, the village was known simply as 'Seton' which is probably a derivative of the words 'Sea' and 'Tun', ie: the village being near to the sea, and tun, meaning a hill or rise. When lands were granted to the Priory of Tynemouth, the name later became known as 'Seton Monachorum', probably to distinguish it from 'Seton Delaval' and 'North Seton'.

The prefix 'Monk' is often found in connection with places belonging to religious houses, and so in this case it later became known as 'Seaton of the Monks' – or Monks Seaton. In the late 13th century, Monkseaton was a substantial village, being one of 10 manors of Tynemouth Priory, having 15 bondsmen, 10 cotmen and 3 freeholds listed in 1292. In 1332 it is recorded that a raid took place on Tynemouthshire and amongst the misdeeds of the raiders it is said that they deliberately mowed the corn at Monkseaton and carried it away.

Its early background was largely agricultural and there is a reference in the 1300s when the Black Death swept the country, virtually fifty percent of the farms in Monkseaton were left untenanted which had a devastating effect on the small community. As the community recovered, it is recorded that by 1539, there were 10 tenants farming in the village.

Appearing on 19th century maps as a compact rural settlement with substantial housing, the basic street layout largely survives and is still represented by Front Street, Back Lane, Percy Terrace, Relton Terrace, Coronation Crescent, Bygate Road, Chapel Lane and Pykerley Road, with remnants of medieval stone walls and buildings throughout the village.

Other than historical references, little has been recorded of Monkseaton, however it is known that it was a place of some importance. Between the years of 1577 and 1742 coal was worked, and in the 17th, 18th and 19th centuries there were several farms along with the usual tradespeople such as blacksmiths, shoemakers and shopkeepers.

In 1663 at a rental of £40 per year, the principal tenant of Monkseaton was a Thomas Mills who held two copyhold farms which contained the following closes: Peckerlaw, Berrishill, Boggpool, Tolls Close, North Ridge, South Ridge, Well Ridge and Town End Field. (Many of these field names are reflected in the present day street names on Red House Farm Estate.) At a rental of £10 per year, a William Otway was also a tenant of land which lay to the south of the village and consisted of four closes known as  the North and South Casetings (or Casetons), the Fatting Pasture and Low Close. The Dunn family rose to prominence during the 1700s and were principal tenants in the village. Successive generations have continued to farm much of the land in Monkseaton since then.

There was a large brewery, and with up to 5 inns, the population which varied between 427 in 1801 rising to 952 by the year 1901, was well catered for with ale!

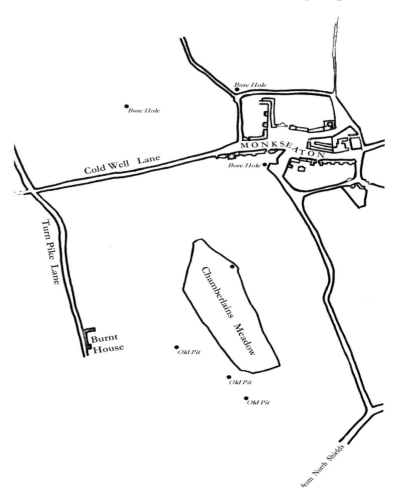

*An early map of Monkseaton, showing the layout of the village and connecting roads c.1833. Locations of old bore holes and pits are also indicated.*

8

The 'Centre' of Monkseaton was, and still is formed by the triangle of land which is evident at the top of Percy Terrace, outside the Black Horse and opposite the front of the Ship Inn. Many people believed that this area was once the site of a Village Green, but this is not the case as Monkseaton has never had a Village Green. The area was simply part of the neighbouring farmland and roads.

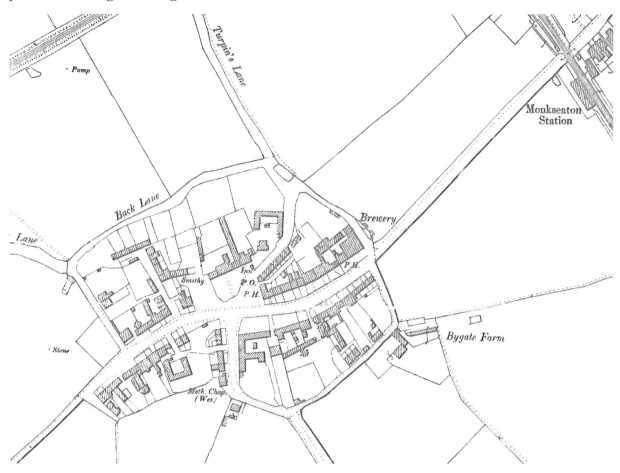

Prior to the Lighting and Watching Act of 1833, there was no police organisation and so the landowners and farmers of the various townships bonded themselves together to form what was known as an 'Association for the Prosecution of Felons'. When any member fell victim to robbery, theft or assault, the association would usually offer a reward for the apprehension of the wrong-doer. When regular policing came about, any outside operations during the hours of darkness requiring more light than that reflected from the cottage windows were conducted by the use of lanterns made of punctured tin containing a tallow dip. Keeping a watchful eye on these activities, was the one village constable; Andrew Todd who also tended the highways. He was succeeded by a PC Hateley.

Post was delivered single-handedly to Whitley, Monkseaton and Hillheads by the village postmistress, Mrs Kipping whose husband tended the fifty street lamps in the district.

Early education tended to be quite a hit and miss affair, with passing references to some kind of school at Bye Gate in 1841, another one in the Fold, a classroom at a room adjoining the Black Horse, and a day school at the little Wesleyan Chapel on Chapel Lane, however, it is understood that many children also attended school at the neighbouring village of Cullercoats until the first established school in the area opened at Whitley in 1870.

Monkseaton developed as a residential centre from the late 1800s and over the past century; it has been slowly absorbed into the urban confines of nearby Whitley Bay, despite much of its history pre-dating that town by many years. During that time, many changes have taken place, most of which have been so gradual that they have simply passed by unnoticed. Housing estates now cover the many fields that once formed part of the local farmland. Trees and hedgerows have been uprooted and cleared to accommodate new and wider roads. Many of the old farmhouses and buildings that once stood in Monkseaton Village have long since disappeared and remain only as distant memories. The rest sadly, have long since been forgotten.

Despite its growth and expansion, all the locals and long term residents of Monkseaton still fondly refer to it as 'The Village'.

*This view of Monkseaton Village is dated 1912, and shows the first Ship Inn (originally built in 1688 as a farmhouse). The inn is visible to the extreme left of the picture alongside East Farm House. Scott & Robson's grocery store at the top of Percy Terrace, has been converted to a house, but is easily recognisable and separated by a narrow lane, standing next to the original 3-storey Black Horse Inn built in 1793.*

## LOCAL WRITERS

Between the century 1800-1900, it is interesting to read how some local writers of the period summed up and described Monkseaton Village:

1811: "Monkseaton is a pleasant village, situated 3 miles north west by north from Tynemouth to which parish it belongs, and contains some well built houses belonging to different gentlemen and farmers. Here are also three Public Houses and one Brewery."

1825: "Monkseaton is a pleasant village, situated 3 miles north west by north from Tynemouth. It contains five Farmholds, a Methodist Meeting House, two Public Houses and a large Brewery belonging to Messrs. Dryden & Co."

1834: "Monkseaton is an irregularly built village of no trade, with the exception of a respectable Brewery belonging to Messrs. Sinclair & Co."

1841: "A spirited little village taking part in a movement for the intellectual advancement of the rural population."

1853: "As I approached the pretty little whitewashed village of Monkseaton from the west side, it was pleasing to hear the incessant tapping of the hammers of the local tinkers. At close hand the people of the place were disappointing. The tinkers were industrious only by fits and starts and did not look upon the village as their particular or cherished abode. They treated it as a sort of workshop and spent much of their time wandering the country, selling their wares and carousing."

1893: "Monkseaton is a pretty little village, formerly the sea town of the monks of Tynemouth. When its garden trees are in full leaf, the village has a very picturesque appearance, situated as it is, on a very slight eminence, and many visitors who wish to combine some of the charms of the country with those of the seaside, patronise it during the summer months."

1907: "We recommend Monkseaton, with a walk to the shore before noon, and a rest after lunch, with a country stroll in the evening. To many people, the rural situation, a little from the Links with the slightly elevated position, forms a strong attraction. Monkseaton Village itself is chiefly of good new houses, but there is sufficient of the old characteristic to make the place interesting as it is quiet and beautiful. Much has been done in the use of foliage to make the district attractive and it is rapidly becoming a charming and popular resort and the chief residential suburb of Newcastle upon Tyne, for such it would seem nature has destined it."

Not all of these colourful descriptions apply today, however there is still a certain charm and character evident in the village.

## MONKSEATON POPULATION

A census is a complete population count for a given area or place taken on a specific date and the 1841 census is considered to be the first modern UK version. However, returns were also submitted before that time, and the earliest count for Monkseaton Village appears to have taken place in 1801.

The table below shows the population of the village from 1801, and how it has gradually increased over the years.

| Date | Population |
|------|-----------|
| 1801 | 427 |
| 1821 | 537 |
| 1831 | 489 |
| 1841 | 581 |
| 1851 | 424 |
| 1861 | 421 |
| 1871 | 453 |
| 1891 | 450 |
| 1901 | 952 |
| 1911 | 2,791 |
| 1921 | 4,639 |
| 1931 | 9,663 |
| 1941 | No Census (Wartime) |
| 1951 | 15,300 |
| 1961 | 18,701 |
| 1971 | 20,047 |
| 1981 | 20,562 |

With the advantages of the new railway, together with modern housing development in the early 1900s, it can be seen that the population of the village almost trebled between 1901 and 1911.

Between the census of 1911 and 1921, Monkseaton combined with Whitley Bay; however it was still possible to determine population numbers for each district.

Monkseaton continued to expand beyond the original village boundary as further housing developed, and new areas included Monkseaton North, South and West with the resulting steady increase in population.

# MONKSEATON FOLK

In the early days, a majority of the village folk were considered to be sober and hard working people, however it was taken for granted that every so often and up to a week at a time, the male element would 'go out on the beer'. The chosen times for these outbreaks were usually at New Year and early springtime when married men were 'hired' and in May or November single servants were 'hired' for the festivities.

At Christmas, it was common for the Earsdon Sword Dancers to visit the village and dance in the lanes wearing white tunics, crimson sashes, velvet knee breeches and buckled shoes. Outside people often flocked into the village to join in the fun or simply watch. It was quite common for music and dancing to follow outside the Ship Inn which carried on until a late hour. Although these festive times were few and far between, it was general for thrifty habits to prevail, with nearly every household in the village laying in adequate food stocks during the summer and autumn months in preparation for the coming winter.

Stocks of herring were bought by the hundred from North Shields when they were cheap, and were carefully preserved and stored in large earthenware jugs or bins. Potatoes too, at a cost of fifteen shillings for a ten stone bag were put aside along with rough and wholesome food and clothing.

The village children were trained to be thrifty and were not encouraged in any way to practise extravagance. During harvest time, many of them worked in the fields harvesting potato and turnip crops while others were expected to take their share in gleaning after the corn had been cut. Wheaten flour which had been gathered was sent to the mill for grinding, and by these means, most families were able to lay up a good stock of food. Clothes were considered to be necessary inasmuch as they brought comfort and warmth. The women mostly made their own or they went to the village dressmaker; Betty Pigg, while the men had theirs made by the village tailor; Joe Blake of The Ship Inn, who commanded much respect and influence. He would visit many of the homes and local farms to give so many days sewing, and his work was considered to be of the finest quality. Joe had a weakness for snuff, and on his daily visits he was also regarded as the 'News Circulator' in the village as he travelled around with his greyhound which had an infallible instinct for rabbits, which ensured that there was always food on his table.

If a native of the village died, then it was expected that every adult would attend the funeral in conventional attire. Every male had to appear in black with a high hat and every female in a black dress, hat and shawl, but where did an ordinary person get a high hat from? The simple answer is that stationmasters were supplied with a new hat each year as part of their uniform, and the old ones could be disposed of or loaned out. Hats which were too big for the owners were stuffed with paper, and those which were too small simply perched precariously on the wearers head. Perhaps there were occasions when some funerals looked more ludicrous than dignified!

References to many of the other characters and people who lived in the village are included in the separate sections throughout this book, and even today, albeit on a slightly different scale there are still many well known characters and people in the village who make their own local contribution.

# MONKSEATON BOUNDARY

Up to the late 1800s, the core of old Monkseaton Village was bounded to the north by Back Lane, to the south by Bygate Lane (Bygate Road), to the west by Pykerley Lane (Pykerley Road) and to the east by Turpin's Lane (Relton Terrace). Beyond this area, it was only fields and farmland which separated the other nearby villages which included Whitley to the east, Cullercoats to the southeast, Preston to the south, Murton to the south west, Earsdon to the west, Holywell to the north west and Hartley to the north, all of which would have then been clearly visible across the open fields. The outline shape of the village perhaps resembles that of a dog's head looking towards the left, and even as the surrounding area has been built up over the years, the original street pattern can still be clearly seen on modern maps.

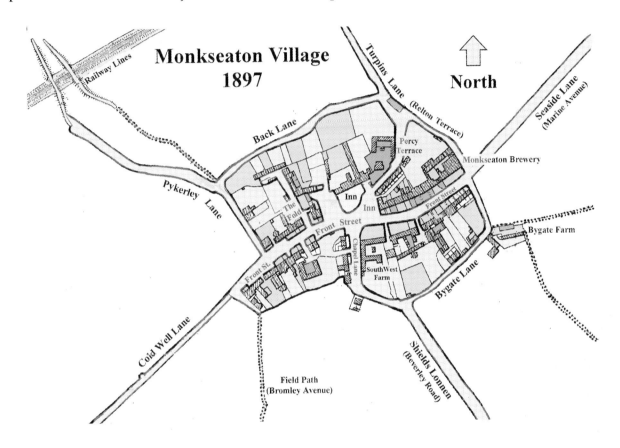

## The Village Boundary

Before traditional bricks were used, thousands of buildings and structures in the North East of England were made from sandstone, which was always in plentiful supply.

By the early 1900s, bricks began to replace sandstone as a building material, and in Monkseaton itself, there are very few original sandstone structures left, however most of what does still exist, lies within the central core of what used to be the old medieval part of the village itself, much of which loosely marks out the boundary of the old village.

As we examine evidence of old stonework, and commencing from the lane which connects Bromley Avenue and Chapel Lane, a rugged sandstone wall adjoins the nearby glazier's premises to form the boundary edge of this pathway, and although the date cannot be confirmed, its origins probably relate to nearby South West Farm. Slightly south of this wall, next to the present clinic, the old Bygate Infants schoolhouse was originally a small single-storey stone-built cottage with a stone outbuilding. The cottage was later converted to include an upper brick-built storey. The ground floor is clearly visible in sandstone with the first floor being rendered in mortar/pebbledash.

Opposite this house, a stone boundary wall which now encloses new apartments, once enclosed South West Farmhouse and stackyard, and was rebuilt in the 1950s when Chapel Lane was widened.

The wall runs the length of Chapel Lane before curving east into Bygate Road where it connects with Garden Cottage, dating to the mid 1700s. The wall then continues on the north side of Bygate Road, and although repaired over the years with rubble and cement rendering, it continues with a short 'gap' to accommodate the terraced cottages (Nos. 6 to 10 Bygate Road) as far as Victoria Place where it extends towards the back of Front Street. The lane, next to a DIY shop bears evidence of old stonework that was once part of the various farm buildings which stood in the middle of the old village, and includes Monkseaton Methodist Church. Crossing to the north side of Front Street, the clean stone-built Monkseaton Cottage is probably the oldest recorded structure in the village. Almost hidden from view to the rear of the present Monkseaton Arms, remnants of the rear section of the old brewery wall become apparent, and reclaimed stonework from the brewery is evident on Relton Terrace where it has been incorporated to form the boundary walls of the modern houses on Relton Place. Interestingly, the foundations of the present houses which comprise Percy Terrace are built on a sandstone base which is evident on close inspection.

*Bygate Schoolhouse in 2004.*

*Garden Cottage, built from sandstone in the mid 1750s, connects with the old boundary stone wall on Bygate Road.*

*The stone wall to the rear of Monkseaton Brewery extends to Percy Terrace, the houses of which are built on sandstone foundations.*

When part of East Farm, (at the top of Percy Terrace) was demolished, some of this stonework was used to construct the triangular wall which stood opposite the Ship pub. Sadly this was removed and used as infill, when the nearby underground public toilets were paved over in 2006. Other stonework which was still evident in the Fold up to the mid 1950s has long since disappeared, however traces of the old village boundary wall are extant on Pykerley Road between Pykerley Mews and Back Lane.

# MONKSEATON PLAN

This plan serves as a reference guide and indicates the locations of some of the streets, buildings and other structures in Monkseaton Village which are referred to throughout this book.

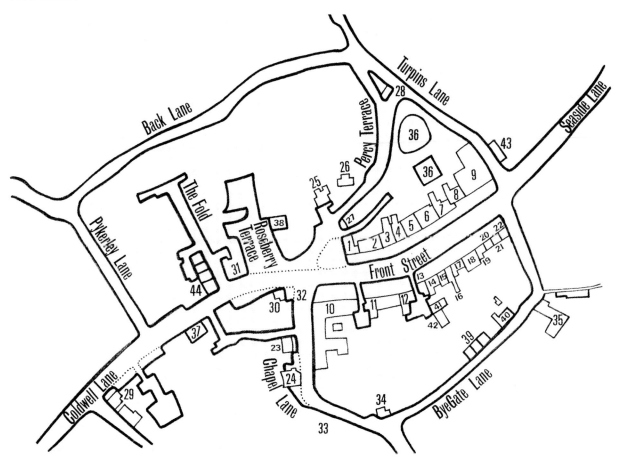

| | |
|---|---|
| 1. Black Horse Inn | 23. Three Horse Shoes/Rose Cottage |
| 2. Coronation Row | 24. Wesleyan Chapel |
| 3. Grid House/Norie Electrical | 25. Old Ship Inn |
| 4. Dwelling Houses | 26. East Farm |
| 5. Monkseaton Cottage | 27. Scott and Robson's Shop |
| 6. Monkseaton House | 28. Cattle Trough |
| 7. Brewery Harness Room | 29. Bromley Place |
| 8. Monkseaton Arms | 30. Village Slaughterhouse |
| 9. Monkseaton Brewery | 31. Seven Stars Inn |
| 10. South West Farm | 32. Blue Billy Stone |
| 11. Methodist Church | 33. Infants School |
| 12. North East Farm (Village Farm) | 34. Garden Cottage |
| 13. North East Farm (Village Farm) | 35. Bygate Farm |
| 14. Holly Cottage | 36. Monkseaton House Reservoirs |
| 15. Ivy Cottage | 37. North Farm |
| 16. Lily Cottage | 38. North West Farm |
| 17. Gourd Cottage | 39. Bygate Cottages |
| 18. Clayton House | 40. Rock Cottage |
| 19. Woodbine Cottage | 41. Seaton House |
| 20. Cottage | 42. Victoria Cottage |
| 21. Cottage | 43. Malting & Brewery Stables |
| 22. Cottage | 44. Fold Cottages |

# FARMS AND FIELDS

## MONKSEATON FARMS

It is difficult to imagine that up to the end of the 1800s, Monkseaton was just a tiny village, surrounded by dozens of fields and farms. To assist in understanding how Monkseaton Village has developed over the years, it is necessary to consider all the associated farms and related outlying fields which were once the hub of the entire community. In 1757, records indicate that the village consisted only of five farm houses; however a field plan based on an old 1850 tithe map shows the boundaries of fourteen different farms.

Over the years, nearly all these farms appear to have retained their original boundaries and show the principle on which division was carried out. For example most of the farm buildings were grouped fairly close together in the village, while the lands attached to them radiate outwards to the edge of the township. The largest; North West Farm once covered an area of over 195 acres and extended north from Cauldwell Lane towards Earsdon Village and the smallest; Bygate Farm covered an area of only 23 acres and was situated to the south of Bygate Road and St Ronan's Road.

Others included East Farm, North East (Village Farm), Red House Farm, North Farm, West Farm, South West Farm, Seatonville Farm, Burnt House Farm, Rake House Farm, South Farm, Hill Heads Farm and Dickies Holm Farm (sometimes referred to as Blacksmiths Farm).

*Red House Farm in 1903. Charlie Dunn is the farmer to the extreme left.*

There are however, many recorded variations in the acreage of these farms over the years, so it is not possible to accurately account for the size of many of them. An area of common land known as Chamberlain's Meadow took in the area now occupied by Monkseaton First School and part of Churchill, Roker and Maple Avenue. Several fields within each area of farmland were given names, which made them easily identifiable to the individual farmers, and many modern street names particularly those on Red House Farm Estate, were derived or named after these fields. Some good examples are; North Ridge, Well Ridge, Tolls Close, Caseton Close and Berris Hill, all of which were once individual fields within the boundary of both North West and South West Farm. In Monkseaton Village, Pykerley Road is a name derived from Far Pickerlaw or Peckerlaw Hill which also stood within the boundary of North West Farm, as well as Hill Field, from nearby North Farm. Some other obvious assumptions can be made from names such as Eastfield, Westfield, Wellfield, Springfield and Closefield etc.

Since 1850, many fields and farms were sold off to accommodate housing and expanding development, as a result of which, some newer and smaller farms came into being. These included Newsteads Farm at West Monkseaton from within the lands of North West Farm, and also Burnt House Nurseries, which were created from the last remaining fields of Burnt House Farm following its demolition in 1929.

Two farms which stood immediately outside the boundary of Monkseaton, are Briar Dene Farm to the north and Murton Steads Farm to the south west. As new roads and streets were laid out in Monkseaton, many of them followed farm and field boundaries and can be identified and traced by a careful comparison between old and modern ordnance survey maps.

16

# BURNT HOUSE FARM

Burnt House Farm was built in 1700, and together with the accompanying farmland, occupied an area of around 112 acres, extending to 160 acres by 1873. The origins of the farm name are unconfirmed, but the obvious suggestion is that it may have derived its name after a fire. The farm was the property of a John Reay, subsequently passing on his death in 1715 to his nephew, Charles Archbold of Monkseaton. The farm remained in the possession of Charles Archbold until 1762 when a moiety was sold by his trustees to a Nathaniel Tavernor of North Shields, with a further moiety being sold in 1815 to a John Crawford of North Shields. It appears that the farm remained in the possession of Nathaniel Tavernor and his descendants until 1902, when it came into the possession of an Alexander Fairweather.

*Burnt House Farmhouse c.1928.*

Throughout the years, the land was farmed by several tenants however the first recorded name was in 1827 and is shown as Elizabeth Fenwick, with the farmer being a Robert Hall. From 1845 to 1851 the tenant was a George Ramsey, followed by a Robert Pye (1851), John Hall (1887), Robert Hall (1889), George Fogg (1897), George Ramsay (1907), C. English (1911 to 1921). In 1929, the farmhouse and accompanying outbuildings were demolished in order to accommodate the new housing development and road widening scheme on Seatonville Road. The farmhouse and outbuildings were situated close to the present junction of Bromley Avenue, on the site of what are now Nos. 64, 66 and 68 Seatonville Road. A narrow path, following the line of the present Bromley Avenue connected Burnt House Farm to Monkseaton Village, through a field which was known as 'The Fleets', part of which still remains to this day, and is generally referred to as 'Bromley Field'. In 1902, the descendants of Nathaniel Tavernor disposed of the property, which came into the possession of an Alexander Fairweather.

*Burnt House Nurseries prior to demolition in 2003.*

*Two stone pillars situated next to 59 Seatonville Road indicate the presence of the old track leading to Burnt House Nurseries and Frankland Mount.*

Burnt House Nurseries, which were situated adjacent to Langley Playing Fields, were created from the last remaining fields of Burnt House Farm following its demolition in 1929. The original access route to these nurseries was via a gate onto a narrow track which ran off Seatonville Road, between the back of what is now Athol and Chatsworth Gardens. Evidence of this track still exists by the presence of two stone pillars which stand directly next to No. 59 Seatonville Road. This track was also at one time the shared access path with a spur leading to Frankland Mount. The entire track and pathway has since been lost to accommodate the extended rear gardens of both Athol and Chatsworth Gardens. Burnt House Nurseries were successfully run as a smallholding for many years by Harry Teasdale, along with his sister; Noel Shand. In 2003, the land was sold to accommodate the Briar Vale housing development.

# BYGATE (MONKSEATON) FARM

Bygate Farm, which dates from 1735, occupied a small triangular area of land, covering what are now the road junctions with Bygate Road, The Gardens and St Ronan's Road. The farm was probably the smallest in Monkseaton, with an adjacent field area of only 24 acres. The earliest recorded owner was a Captain Christopher Spanton who purchased two cottages in Monkseaton during this year, which later became Bygate Farm buildings. One of the cottages was converted to become a stable and cow-house. Christopher Spanton died in London in 1753. The farm remained in the possession of his heirs, and was sold by their representatives in 1795 to an Alexander Crighton of North Shields. By 1851, the tenant of Bygate Farm is recorded as a Joseph Dunn, who also farmed the adjoining North Farm with one labourer. In May 1876, Bygate Farm was offered for sale, and purchased for the sum of £5,050 by a Mr Harvey, to be farmed by Richard Heckles Nesbitt of West Park, Hill Heads and from about 1891 by a John Nicholson. On Wednesday 13th December 1899, the farm was again offered for sale by public auction at the Central Station Hotel, Newcastle. Bidding commenced at £6,000 advancing to only £6,750, so the property was withdrawn and later offered for sale by private treaty. The last two tenant farmers at Bygate were W. Parker in 1911 and Henry Nicholson in 1914. Much of the land was later sold for development as a freehold building estate; however the farm buildings remained until the early 1950s when they were demolished by a William Griffiths who built the bungalow which now stands on this site.

*Right: 1899 Sale Notice for Bygate Farm.*

**Particulars**
AND
## CONDITIONS OF SALE
RELATING TO
# FREEHOLD PROPERTY
KNOWN AS THE
## "BYGATE FARM"
AT MONKSEATON NORTHUMBERLAND
WHICH WILL BE OFFERED FOR
### SALE BY AUCTION
IN
No. 4 Room of the Central Station Hotel, Newcastle-on-Tyne,
ON
*Wednesday, the 13th day of December, 1899,*
AT 3 O'CLOCK IN THE AFTERNOON,
BY
# Mr. R.M. TATE, Auctioneer.

**PARTICULARS**

The Freehold Estate known as "Bygate Farm," situate at Monkseaton, Northumberland, and containing 24.305 acres, or over 117,636 square yards of ripe **Building Land**, with the **Farm** and **Dairy Buildings** thereon.

The valuable land is situate near the Monkseaton Junction of the North-Eastern Railway between Newcastle, North Shields and Blyth. About 64 trains per day enter and leave Monkseaton Station, including 22 expresses, and there are about 26 trains on Sundays.
This service is likely to be largely augmented when the alterations now in progress to connect New Bridge Street and Central Stations are completed, and the circular trains from Newcastle Central to Newcastle Central via Tynemouth, Monkseaton, Jesmond &c., are running.
The Land has extensive frontages to the road between North Shields and Blyth, &c. The Golf Links, the Cliffs, and the Sands are within easy walks, and charming drives are to be had along the coast in view of the sea, and headlands and country scenery ; also places of historic interest. Very choice and uninterrupted views, both of the coast line and the adjoining countryside, may be had from all parts of the estate. The land is on a gentle slope, and well adapted for economical drainage and laying out, being about 120 feet above sea level.

The enormous expansion of Whitley and Monkseaton has almost taken up all other choice available land and several applications have already been made to the owners with a view to immediate building.

The National Electric Traction Company have in hand the construction of an Electric Railway from the Ship Inn, Whitley to the Market Place and Ferries, North Shields.

The Whitley terminus is within a few minutes' walk of the estate, thus giving a direct communication with the river Tyne and the various towns and industries on its banks.

The tenant, Mr Nicholson will allow inspection.

Copies of these Particulars and Conditions may be obtained from C. J. R. BROWN, Esq. LL.B., Solicitor, 33 Saville Street, North Shields ; or from the AUCTIONEER, Victoria Chambers, 98, Howard Street, North Shields.

*Bygate Farm and the old boundary wall 1903.*

# CHAMBERLAIN'S MEADOW

Chamberlains Meadow dates back to at least 1550, and was an area of Common Land which was once farmed by the whole township of Monkseaton for a rent of £1 6s 8d. It has not been established why this meadow was so named. The meadow (superimposed on the modern map) was sandwiched between the lands of South Farm and Seatonville Farm and contained an area of 9 acres, 2 roods and 20 perches and was originally reached by a footpath leading from the west end of Monkseaton Village which roughly followed the line of the present Bromley Avenue towards Burnt House Farm. In 1893, the meadow is recorded as being in the tenure of a Mr George Davison.

As can be seen, most of the meadow was lost to the development of Seatonville Housing Estate in the late 1940s.

# DICKIES HOLM (BLACKSMITHS) FARM

The earliest record of Dickies Holm Farm dates to 1845, when it is recorded as being in the possession of a Mr William Brown, a retired blacksmith, who part-owned and part-

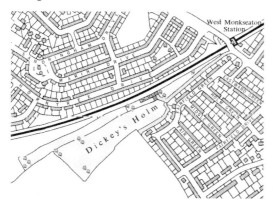

rented the land. The origins of the unusual name are not known however the name 'Holm' is derived from old Norse and was a common element in field names, usually referring to a water meadow, riverside land or a section of dry land in a fen. By 1881 the farm had changed hands, and from this date until 1903 the farmer was a Thomas Charlton, a working blacksmith, and hence the farm was sometimes locally referred to as; 'Blacksmiths Farm'. The farm was situated on a narrow triangular area of land, 10 acres in extent to the west of Earsdon Road, opposite the present West Monkseaton Station and the farmland ran parallel to the south side of the present railway line.

A small stream which separated the townships of Monkseaton and Earsdon, ran the length of the farmland, and was dammed at the entrance, beside Earsdon Road. By 1914 the farmer was an Edward D. Charlton, which by 1938, had changed to J. Todd, a coal merchant, and by the 1960s the land was farmed by a Donald Shaw, who utilised much of the land as nursery gardens. He also ran three greengrocery stores in the Monkseaton and Whitley Bay areas which were situated at 69 Park View, Whitley Bay, 38 Ilfracombe Gardens and 97 Cauldwell Lane, Monkseaton which is where much of his local produce was sold. Earsdon Road, which crosses the railway line at West Monkseaton was also occasionally referred to as 'Dickies Holm Bridge'. The farmhouse and outbuildings were demolished in the 1980s and the land has remained undeveloped, however a section of this land adjacent to the railway line is occasionally used as a maintenance base for the Metro system.

*The old track leading from West Monkseaton towards Dickies Holm Farm.*

# EAST FARM

East Farm and its outbuildings stood slightly to the east of the present Ship Inn on the corner of what is now Percy Terrace and Lyndhurst Road and probably dates to the 1600s. Originally the home of a Henry Nicholson, the first record of the building appears in 1710 when it was surrendered by a John Mills together with the principal part of the stackyard to his son, John Mills. The Mills family were at this time, prominent land and property owners in the village. By 1757, East Farm was shown to

be in the possession of a Henry Hudson Esq. It is recorded that during the 1800s whilst some wallpaper was being removed from a room in the farmhouse, a large oil painting was found on a stone above a chimney-piece. The painting was said to be in a 'remarkable state of preservation', and depicted a ruined castle on a hill surrounded by trees. Nothing further is known of this picture. In another room, a romantic legend was found scratched on a

*East Farmhouse is the building situated next to the original Ship Inn near the top of Percy Terrace.*

glass window pane which read: 'John Bennet, Margaret Hall, 1796 – Lovers'. Sadly nothing is known of this couple.

Between 1827 to sometime after 1841, the tenant of East Farm was recorded as an Ann Nixon, which for many years thereafter was locally referred to as 'Nixon's Farm'. A well which stood close to East Farm was known as 'Nixon's Well' or 'Nixon's Pond'

and could be topped up and fed by diverting the water course running from the higher Cold Well. This pond was regularly used as the watering place for cattle and horses. Another well which stood in a nearby field and known as the 'Far Well' was occasionally used when other water supplies failed.

*The former stackyard of East Farm, following demolition in 1961. The houses of Percy Terrace are in the background.*

Other tenant farmers over the years have included: Percival Wright (1851), Thomas Wright (1871), William Nesbit (1887), William Harrett (1889), John Nellis (1899) and Henry James (1924).

The farmhouse was uninhabited during 1881, and the site was demolished and cleared in 1961 to make way for new housing on Percy Terrace under the name of Relton Place.

# FANCY FIELDS

A reference is made to Fancy Fields in William Weaver Tomlinson's book: *Historical Notes on Cullercoats, Whitley and Monkseaton* which was first published in 1893, but the origins of this colourful field name remain a mystery. In order to walk from Whitley to Monkseaton Village during the 1800s, it was necessary to follow a pretty country field path through the centre of a field known as Whitley Nook, which closely followed the course of the present Norham Road. This path then crossed directly over the old railway lines emerging at a point close to the present 90° 'curve' in the road at what is now Marmion Terrace and St Ronan's Road. It was this point which formed the edge of South or Village Field, more affectionately known as 'Fancy Field' – a part of North East or 'Village Farm'.

Immediately after crossing the old railway lines, the pathway continued and ran

*Fancy Field is superimposed on this map. Within the field boundary, a spring, known as the 'Fancy Well' occupied a position roughly midway along the front of the present Osborne Gardens.*

between two wooden gates towards the south eastern corner of Monkseaton Village, closely following the route of what later became St Ronan's Road.

Studying this 1893 illustration by Thomas Eyre Macklin, we have our back to the railway lines, looking west from a point close to what is now the corner of Marmion Terrace and St Ronan's Road. Bygate Farm buildings can be seen at the far end of the pathway, and the remaining structures and hedgerow follows the line of Coronation Crescent. The large whitewashed building and tall chimney to the right belong to Monkseaton Brewery on Front Street. It is recorded that in 1816 a small Methodist chapel, measuring 12 yards by 6 yards was built on the south east corner of Monkseaton Village on the edge of Fancy Fields, close to the junction of what is now St Ronan's Road and Coronation Crescent. Little information has been recorded of this chapel, which by the early 1890s was in ruins. It is probable that this was the first Methodist place of Worship to be built in the district, and records suggest that it was built by eight men – *'all of Tynemouth'*. The names are not significant; however one of these names is, as it refers to a John Dunn, which may be connected to the inscription carved on a stone on the nearby Rock Cottage. It is likely that services were held in this chapel until the replacement was built in Chapel Lane in 1843.

Horses and cattle grazed freely on 'Fancy Field' which disappeared when the course of the present railway line and new station were laid out, followed by the early 1900s housing development which comprised Kensington Gardens, Kenilworth Road, Waverley Avenue and Melrose Avenue. The old field path was built up to eventually become St Ronan's Road.

*Looking west through Fancy Fields, Monkseaton. This picture is a watercolour painted by local artist, John Falconar Slater. The field path which later became St Ronan's Road is visible to the left, beyond which are Bygate Farm buildings. The hedgerow in the distance forms the eastern edge of Coronation Crescent leading to the corner of Front Street. Monkseaton Brewery with its tall chimney is the large white building towards the right of the picture.*

## HILL HEADS FARM

The earliest record of Hill Heads Farm goes back to 1757 when it was recorded as being in the possession of a John Boulby and the heirs of a W. Johnson. The farmland was recorded as being 84 acres in extent and was situated on the south eastern boundary of Monkseaton Township, where much of the land incorporated the northern extremity of Marden Limestone Quarry. The farm buildings stood south east of Hill Heads Road, close to where Lovaine Avenue and the present school is now situated. Tenant farmers since 1841 have included Robert Thompson, who was succeeded by a Thomas Thompson from around 1871 until the early 1900s. Thomas Thompson was well known in the area and nicknamed 'The Grand Old Man' or 'Father of Whitley' because of his long service to the local Council and was the first chairman of the town's Board of Guardians. Thomas was also related to the Gofton family of Monkseaton (*see Gofton's section*). On the occasion of his 85th birthday, a complimentary dinner was held at the Victoria Hotel, Whitley Bay. He died in October the following year, 1911 and was buried in St Paul's Churchyard, Whitley Bay. In 1875, the south eastern section of land adjacent to Hill Heads Road was taken over by a Richard Heckels Nesbit who set up and utilised the area with steam brickworks which continued for a period of fourteen years, before being landscaped in 1889 to create market gardens which were later taken over and run by the Steel Family. In 1914, a school (now Marden Bridge School) was built on part of the land; Lovaine Avenue and Hotspur Avenue were also laid out along with a council depot and abattoir.

Complimentary Dinner
To Thos. Thompson, Esq.
HILL HEADS, WHITLEY BAY,
*On the occasion of his 85th Birthday.*

MONDAY, JANUARY 10TH, 1910
AT THE VICTORIA HOTEL, WHITLEY BAY

Chairman—William Spicer, Esq., J.P.
Vice-Chairman—James Hilton, Esq.

The depot and abattoir were replaced with housing during the 1980s and 1990s.

*Hill Heads Farm c.1900. The group of men pictured have gathered to play a game of quoits which was always a popular game during this era. Thomas Thompson is in the centre of the photograph, holding a stick.*

# NORTH FARM

Very few records exist in relation to North Farm, the lands of which were situated to the north side of Monkseaton Village. The actual farmhouse however, stood on the south side of Front Street on the site of the present 'Homeprior House'. The earliest record is dated 1757 when it was in the possession of a Mr Thompson. Subsequent tenants and farmers are shown as Joseph Dunn in 1855, Robert Scott in 1887 and William Mitchison in 1897. A sale notice advertises the farm to be sold by auction, at the Commercial Hotel, Howard Street, North Shields on Tuesday 13th June 1865 at six o'clock in the evening. A colourful description of the farm is described in the notice shown right. The last recorded tenant farmer in 1907 is shown as a Joseph Dunn however records suggest that the later occupants of the old farmhouse in 1915 were; T.T. Gofton (Builder) and in 1921, Edward Gray (Coal Merchant). The farmhouse and adjoining buildings were eventually converted to incorporate what was later to become the 'Coast Builders Merchants'. Demolished in 1985, the site later accommodated sheltered housing called 'Homeprior House', however the farmland which had disappeared many years earlier accommodated much of the housing to the north side of Monkseaton.

*Left: The stone lintel above the door of the house bears the inscription 'North Farm'.
Some interesting comparisons can be made with this photograph and the one below of the Coast Builders Merchants, seen here under demolition in 1985. The tarpaulins at the end of the building are covering the remains of the above house. The original brick archway (above) was incorporated to form the portico seen below. The double upper floor windows are evident on both pictures.*

# NORTH EAST or MONKSEATON VILLAGE FARM

Occasionally referred to as North East Farm, records indicate that Monkseaton Village Farm has existed since 1660. Simply known as 'Village Farm', the farmhouse and outbuildings stood in the central core of the village on the area situated between the Methodist Church and Alder Court. During 1899 the byres and stables of Village Farm were converted to become the present Methodist Church and many of its original outbuildings still exist which, over the years have been used as a garage, a taxi office, and a printers. Early records indicate that the farm was surrendered in 1680 by an Elizabeth Collyer of Newcastle to a Robert Cay of Newcastle – a baker and brewer. The lands of Village Farm extended north east of the village and included a parcel of land known as 'Clay Bank Close', on which Monkseaton Colliery was situated, with coal being worked until the year 1720 when it was said that the colliery was 'wholly wrought out'. The *Newcastle Courant* dated 8th February 1755 advertised: *'The main coal in the Clay Bank Close, nigh Monk Seaton, the same being six quarters deep clean coal and clear of water'*, to be let.

*The Byres and outbuildings of Village Farm soon after conversion to an Anglican Chapel*

This area is now occupied by the streets of Shaftesbury Avenue, Grasmere Crescent and part of Davison Avenue. A survey of 1757 indicated that the farmland of Village Farm measured 106 acres in extent with ownership under the heirs of a John Cay Esquire. From 1827 until at least 1884, the tenant of Village Farm is recorded as a Henry Dunn with the farmhouse then described as having a spacious stone-flagged kitchen at the front with a passage leading to the back kitchen. To the west of the house, next to South West Farm stood the byres, turnip house and outbuildings which were later converted to an Anglican Chapel. A passageway or narrow lane led to a small cottage which overlooked the farmyard and was occupied by a Betty Pigg and her daughter who was the village dressmaker. Milk produced on Village Farm was placed into barrels and sealed with a cork bung. The barrels were then slung onto each side of an ass and transported by the animals to North Shields. The farmer, Henry Dunn, had a dispensing agent in North Shields from where the milk would be distributed and sold. In later years, carts were provided which were drawn along by ponies to carry out this task. Towards the end of 1845, Monkseaton Village farmhouse was completely rebuilt and still stands immediately to the east of the Methodist Church. In 1884, the farm was offered for sale by public auction at the Central Station Hotel, Newcastle and came into the possession of a Mr T.A. Potts of Newcastle who laid out a majority of the lands for building purposes.

## NORTH WEST FARM (NEWSTEADS FARM)

*Newsteads Farm House c.1930.*

North West Farm was once the largest farm in Monkseaton and occupied a majority of the lands to the west side of the village. It was during the early 1900s that most of these fields became better known as Newsteads Farm. Access to the original farm buildings and fields was via a bridle path known as Pykerley Lane (now built up as Pykerley Road). The farmland was bounded to the east by fields belonging to Red House Farm and North Farm. The earliest references of North West Farm date back to 1632 when the owner was recorded as a John Mills of Bishopwearmouth followed in 1663 by a Thomas Mills. In 1690, the property was surrendered and came into the possession of a Henry Hudson of Whitley. Subsequent tenant farmers have included the following: John Mills (1757), Thomas Dunn (1800), Zephaniah Shipley (1808), William Clark (1816), John Wight (1827), Henry Davison (1851). In 1853 the property was sold by the representatives of Henry Hudson (1690) to the Duke of Northumberland. From 1855, John Nicholson was the tenant, followed by Henry Nicholson in 1887 who ran the farm until at least 1921 with an interesting report in the *Shields Daily News* stating that on 22nd April 1907, Henry Nicholson was charged with selling deficient milk.

On Saturday 6th August 1892, Monkseaton (North West) Farm was offered for sale by public auction at the County Hotel, Newcastle. The description stated that the farmland measured 236 acres in extent which are understood to have included the buildings sometimes referred to as Monkseaton Dairy Farm which stood on the extremities of the fields close to the Fold and Rosebery Terrace, Monkseaton. A further notice dated Friday 16th April 1920 advertised a small section of the land and property for sale by auction at the County Hotel as follows: '*In the Village of Monkseaton, the Dwelling House formerly attached to Northwest Farm situate in the centre of the village, containing seven rooms, with numerous outbuildings and a considerable area of ground in the front and rear, the whole extending to about 7,500 square yards.*' The property was sold to a Mr Lambert of Gateshead for the sum of £3,000 and were demolished three years later in 1923 to make

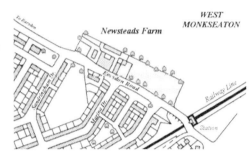

way for the construction of the present Ship Inn. Tenant farmers on this section are recorded as follows: Joseph Wright (1827), Henry Davison (1855), Henry and John Nicholson (1887), Henry Davison (1907). By 1915, this house was in the occupation of an E. Gray, a coal merchant. In 1901, Newsteads Farmhouse and outbuildings were constructed adjacent to Earsdon Road to serve as a replacement for the original farm buildings in Monkseaton. Since then, and over subsequent years, almost all the farm fields and outbuildings which became Newsteads have been lost to housing development, however the actual farmhouse still exists and is now a private dwelling house. A notice dated 1920, offered Newsteads Farm for sale by auction at the County Hotel, Newcastle and the farm residence is described as containing a Drawing Room, Dining Room, Breakfast Room, Five Bedrooms, Two Attics, Bathroom, Kitchen, Pantry, Dairy, Laundry and Out-Offices with a Fruit and Vegetable Garden. The Farm Homestead included; A Two-stall Pony Stable, Hay House, Coach House, Cart Shed, Harness Room, Seven-stall Work

*Monkseaton Dairy Farm under demolition in 1923. The Ship Inn now stands on this site.*

Stable, Loose Box, Fold of three eyes, Turnip House, Byre for 24 Cows, Hutch for 6 Calves, Bull House, Meal House, Corn Barn, Threshing Barn, Large Hay Shed, Shed for Long Carts, Chaff House, Poultry House, Two Piggeries, Workshop, 3 Loose Boxes convertible into Byres for 8 Cows, Byre for 16 Cows and Turnip House. The sale included Two Cottages containing Three and Two Rooms respectively with Out-Offices and incorporated 189 Acres of Arable and old grassland. The lot was sold to the Backworth Coal Company on 14th April 1920 for the sum of £15,000 where in 1948 almost all of the land was taken over for a five year period as open cast workings.

Prior to the development of the southwesterly section of Red House Farm Estate, the farmhouse, outbuildings and remaining land were taken over by North Tyneside Council Parks Department and developed as Nursery Gardens concentrating on the production of plants. The first block of greenhouses was built in 1972 with over 14,000 square feet of glass being used. The council vacated the site in the 1990s when the farm outbuildings were demolished to make way for new housing development.

*Right: Newsteads Farm buildings, Earsdon Road c. 1970.*

# RAKE HOUSE FARM

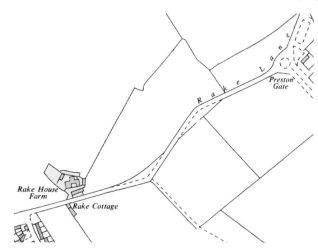

Although not strictly within the boundary of Monkseaton, Rake House Farm adjoined the lands of Seatonville Farm to the extreme south west of the township.

Farm buildings stood on both sides of Rake Lane, close to the present North Tyneside General Hospital, however only the farmhouse situated on the north side of the road now survives. The first record of Rake House Farm goes back to 2nd April 1662 when the property was surrendered by a Thomas Hall to Ralph Grey, eventually passing to one of his descendents – Ralph William Grey of Backworth who was a principal landowner in this area. The land comprised an area of 120 acres. In 1822, along with his Backworth Estate, Ralph William Grey sold Rake House Farm and its land to the Duke of Northumberland. Tenant farmers since 1822 have included: Thomas Fenwick (1841), Joseph Fenwick (1845), Joseph and William Fenwick (1855), William Dunn (1871), Joseph Dunn (1887), Joseph Fenwick (1907). The *Shields Daily News* dated 22nd December 1884 carries a report of a huge fire at Rake House Farm which occurred the previous day, and completely destroyed sixteen stacks, and a large proportion of the season's stored crops. All the livestock was saved. A further fire was also reported in the stackyard of the farm on 2nd January 1912.

From February 1948, most of the land lying adjacent to Rake House Farm was taken over for short term Open Cast Coal Mining which continued for almost two years.

*Looking east on Rake Lane towards the Foxhunters, this 1920s photo shows Rake House Farm to the left and Rake Cottage to the right. North Tyneside General Hospital and part of Chirton Grange Estate now occupy most of this area.*

Holloway Bros were contracted to operate the site on behalf of the National Coal Board. When the land was eventually reclaimed in late 1949 through to the 1950s, farming was scaled down and the premises operated as a smallholding and farm shop until the early 2000s when the original farmhouse and outbuildings were sold for development. In 2008, the old farmhouse underwent intensive renovation work. The outbuildings and stackyard were completely rebuilt, modernised and converted to accommodate a series of small offices and business units. The only other significant development to take place on the lands of Rake House Farm was that which accommodated the re-alignment, straightening and widening of the adjacent Rake Lane during the 1970s.

*In 1948, Open Cast Mining is well under way on the lands adjoining Rake House Farm.*

## RED HOUSE FARM

Probably one of the better known, but smaller farms in the area was Red House Farm which was split into two portions, connected by a short pathway between. It would

*Red House Farm c.1930, taken from an old water colour painting.*

appear that during the 1600s and 1700s, these lands were possibly separate entities. The lands, which are recorded as measuring between 117 and 125 acres in extent stood slightly north west of the village on the area which is now occupied by part of Beaumont Park Housing Estate, Whitley Bay High School and the adjacent allotment gardens behind Deneholm and Alder Grove. The actual farmhouse and stackyard were situated at what is now the rear of Southridge First School between the end of Earnshaw Way and Chevington Grove. (Despite what may be otherwise suggested by the name, the nearby Red House Farm Housing Estate was actually built completely within the adjoining lands of neighbouring North West Farm, and not on the lands of Red House Farm.)

To reach Red House Farm from the village, it was necessary to pass Monkseaton Brewery and travel for approx one mile along Turpin's Lane (Relton Terrace). The earliest records go back to 1687, when on the 16th August that year; the farm was surrendered by the owners to a John Clark of North Shields. Subsequent owners and tenants of the North Portion over the following years included; William Reay (1698), Charles Archbold (1715), Samuel Lacy (1757), Thomas Wright (1801), William Crawford (1811), John Moor (1841), John Moor Jnr. (1873), Edward Dodds Stobbs (1887), Charles Dunn (1897). Owners and tenants of the South Portion of Red House Farm indicate that on 27th March 1704, six fields were surrendered by a William Wall of Newcastle to a Jonathan Hyndmer.

*This photograph was taken c.1899 and shows the farmer; Charles Robson Dunn and his wife Agnes with their family in the garden of Red House Farm.*

In 1723, the farm was once again surrendered to a Reynolds Hall of Newbiggin and a John Hall Jnr. of Cullercoats.

In 1746, the tenant is recorded as Henry Dunn and by 1757 it was in the possession of Samuel Lacy who was also the owner of the North Portion of the farm. In 1763, the representatives of Jonathan Hyndmer sold the farm to an Anthony Pearson of North Shields which eventually passed under his will to William Linskill of Tynemouth House. The southern section was sold in 1875 to Edward Dodds Stobbs who already owned the North Portion, and it would appear that the farm was merged into single ownership from thereon.

Since 1897, the Dunn family continued to farm the land, which in later

*Charlie Dunn was the last farmer at Red House, and is pictured standing at the gates of the farm here in 1962.*

years included a horse-riding school. Most of the farmland eventually disappeared under the housing development of the 1960s and 70s. Over the years, the Dunn Family became a very prominent farming family in the area, and along with the related Nicholson family, their name features frequently with periodic tenancies of many of the other farms in Monkseaton Village.

# SEATONVILLE FARM

Seatonville Farm, dates back to at least 1625 under the name; Seaton Villa, and during the mid 1800s, the farmland occupied an area of about 110 acres – much the same extent as nearby Burnt House Farm. The name eventually changed to Seaton Ville, and in later years was corrupted to become a single word; Seatonville. The first recorded owner was a Robert Fyfe who surrendered the property on 26th April 1654 to a James Barker of Monkseaton. The farm eventually passed by inheritance to James Barkers' grandson – Robert Barker, a Tanner of Monkseaton Village, and on 27th April 1706, it was surrendered by him to a George Johnson of Monkseaton. By 1757, the property is recorded as being in the possession of the heirs of a William Johnson and in 1792 was sold to a Henry Mitcalfe of Murton House, with a further undated sale to a J. Love of Durham. In 1799, the tenant was recorded as a John Aynsley, and during this year, several thefts of poultry

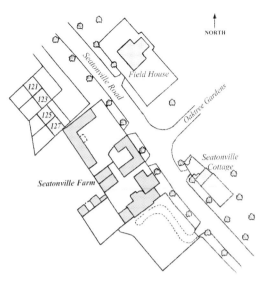

*A plan, showing the location of Seatonville Farm buildings in relation to the present houses.*

occurred. A reward of two guineas was offered by the Tynemouth Association for the Prosecution of Felons to anyone who could give information leading to the conviction of the thieves. John Aynsley is still recorded as the tenant in 1827 followed by Fenwick Aynsley (1841), Francis Hansell (1871), Thomas Dobinson (1881), John & Jane

Dobinson (1898), Josiah & Jane Dobinson (1914). Tom Close of Preston farmed the land from 1921 until sometime after 1940, and he is recorded as the last tenant there. Seatonville Farm existed for just over 330 years until the last of the farm buildings were demolished in 1959 to accommodate new housing, to the west side of the road. Nos. 129 to 147 Seatonville Road were built on the site of the original farm buildings and stackyard. Monkseaton High School also occupies part of this farmland.

*Seatonville Farmhouse, shortly before demolition in 1959.*

*Above: Looking North on Seatonville Road, the main farmhouse is visible to the left, and two terraced farm cottages stood on the opposite side of the road, one of which was demolished in the 1920s to facilitate the widening of Seatonville Road, however the remaining cottage still stands to this day, and is now the only remaining evidence of Seatonville Farm.*

# SOUTH WEST FARM

Out of a total of fourteen recorded farms in Monkseaton, South West Farm was one of the smaller ones. The farm dates from the early 1700s, and occupied an area of almost 244 acres of land, however many documents relating to this farm are missing or incomplete, so details tend to be very sketchy and confusing. As a result, a number of calculated assumptions have been made. Although modernised and altered over the years, most of the actual farm buildings still exist, with the largest sections standing on the corner of Front Street and Chapel Lane, forming what is now a large convenience store. Details taken from a 1757 and an 1850 tithe map indicate that the farmland radiated outwards to the south west, roughly in a triangular shape from Chapel Lane, and encompassed the area now enclosed by Front Street, Cauldwell Lane, Seatonville Road and Bromley Avenue. It also included a square of land to the west of Seatonville Road, enclosed by the present housing built between Cauldwell Avenue and Athol Gardens to the boundary which includes Langley Playing Fields. Another tithe plan dated 1870 records the same fields under the name of 'Monkseaton Farm', however the plan also indicates that the fields extending south towards Hill Heads and recorded under the title of South Farm, also formed part of South West Farm. It is therefore probable that the two farms were generally considered in whole as 'South West Farm'. The earliest records show that in

*South West Farm buildings in the 1940s. The trees were removed soon after this picture was taken, and despite considerable changes over the years, the structures are still easily recognisable. The building in the foreground is now a convenience store.*

1711, the farm was surrendered by a William Hills, to a John Robinson of Whitley, Several changes of ownership and tenants are recorded over subsequent years which include:

    1757; The heirs of a William Johnson.
    1779; William Clark of Dockwray Square, North Shields.
    1813; Ralph Crawford of Hartley South Farm.
    1818; John Moor of Morpeth High House (son-in-law of Ralph Crawford).
    1851; John Nicholson (Tenant Farmer).
    1871; Robert Chater (Tenant Farmer).

On 22nd March 1884, South West Farm was offered for sale by public auction at the Central Station Hotel, Newcastle, and was described as: "A valuable copyhold estate with cottages adjoining", however, a plan of the farmland shows only those lands which were recorded under the title of South Farm.

The outcome of the auction is unclear, but in 1885 it was sold by the representatives of John Moor to the Duke of Northumberland. In 1895, the tenant farmer is recorded as a John Appleby and the *Shields Daily News* carried a report of a large stackyard fire at the premises during that year. By 1921, it was farmed by John Potts, followed in 1926 by Percy Potts and finally by Robson Potts from 1938. By 1949, the farm was no longer in use, and the main buildings on the corner of Front Street and Chapel Lane were taken over during this year by an old established Monkseaton building firm: Gofton Bros., who converted the buildings for retail purposes. *(See section on Gofton's.)*

In later years, the premises were once again altered and adapted to become a small supermarket which subsequently traded as Hintons, Presto, Safeway and the Spar group. The actual farmhouse of South West Farm still exists, and is situated behind the supermarket within the original stackyard, just off Chapel Lane, to the rear of Bygate Road. When Chapel Lane was widened in 1952, the old stackyard wall was demolished and rebuilt slightly to the east, and now encloses new housing apartments –

*The entrance to South West Farm House was through a gated entrance on Chapel Lane. (Photo c.1960)*

Churchill Court. The stone buildings adjoining the Spar shop on Chapel Lane have undergone a number of different uses over the years, including workshop facilities, storage, garaging and offices.

## WEST (GRANGE) FARM

West Farm, (sometimes referred to as Monkseaton Grange Farm) comprised only a small area of land to the south west of the village. Consisting only of four fields, the land encompassed the area now bounded by Earsdon Road, Cauldwell Avenue, Monks Road and Fairfield Drive. Tenant farmers over the years have included: Josiah Dobinson (1887), Matthew Potts (1900), Henry Dunn (1907). The Potts family took over and ran the farm from around 1914 to sometime after 1924 and appear to be the last recorded tenants of the property. The farmland was sold for housing development, and by 1937, the old farmhouse was replaced by the Grange Hotel (later renamed as the Hunting Lodge).

*Above: The area of West Farm is superimposed on this modern map.*

*Left: The corner boundary of West Farm was later developed with the familiar buildings on Earsdon Road and Cauldwell Avenue, shown on this 1970s photograph.*

# STREETS
## MONKSEATON, WHITLEY & HILL HEADS

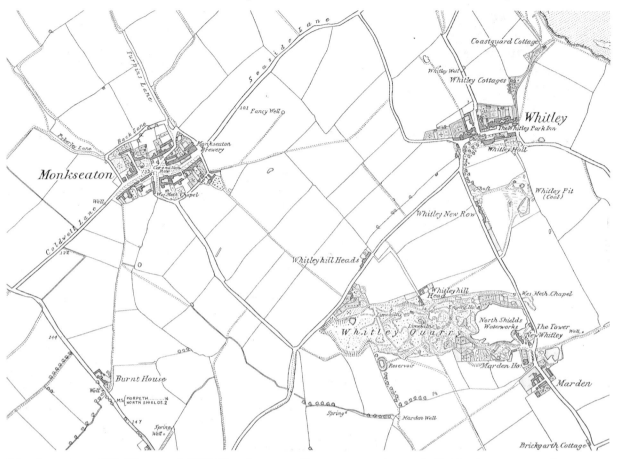

Monkseaton, Whitley and Hill Heads were three separate and distinct areas as shown on this 1856 map. Virtually all the visible fields have since been built over with housing, and although the core pattern of both Monkseaton and Whitley Village still exist, the remaining streets which form the basis of the present day layout of today's main roads are remarkably evident. As can be seen, the Limestone Quarry (typically referred to as Marden Quarry) originally embraced a large area from Whitley Hill Heads to Marden between what is now Shields Road and the Broadway. Around 1875 the western section of the quarry incorporated kilns and was set up by a Richard Heckels Nesbitt as steam brickworks. By 1889 the brickworks had been exhausted and were landscaped to become 'West Park'. The remaining land later came into the possession of the North Shields Waterworks and in more recent years was landscaped to become a countryside park. Early maps indicate that an old waggonway once ran from Marden Limestone Quarry, roughly shadowing the route of the present Broadway to the west. The track then crossed Spital Dene at Tynemouth and terminated at the Low Light Staithes, North Shields. The line of the original Broadway runs to the south of Whitley Village, past Marden Tower which was once a powder store for the quarry. Coal was mined to the north of Monkseaton, and a pit was sunk at Hill Heads. Whitley Colliery stood on the area

*Marden Quarry c.1902.*

between Marden Road South and Plessey Crescent to the west of Whitley Station and the present railway line. Various wells and springs were dotted throughout many of the fields and were once an important source for the supply of fresh water. Perhaps the most notable of these were the 'Fancy Well' which stood in fields now built over as Osborne Gardens, and the 'Cold Well' which was situated by Cauldwell (Coldwell)

Lane near to Pykerley (Lane) Road, each of which are referred to elsewhere in this book. Other smaller wells and springs stood on the lands of Burnt House Farm, Seatonville Farm and the fields now built up as Marden Estate. There was also 'Whitley Well' which stood close to the present junction of Park Road and Park Avenue. Typically, many of the field paths, mostly shown as dotted lines later formed the basis of many of the streets in the area, including Bromley Avenue, Pykerley Road, Relton Terrace, Beverley Road, The Gardens and St Ronan's Road etc. From these early beginnings, the area that we know best today has developed.

*These Pit Cottages were known as Whitley New Row, and stood on the eastern side of what is now Marden Road South, between Felton and Chollerford Avenue. The view looks south towards the Broadway.*

## STREET DEVELOPMENT

As early as 1888, plans had been drawn up for housing development immediately to the east of the old village street boundary. The plan shown below indicates that Marine Avenue was to become a continuation of Monkseaton Front Street, commencing at the junction with Relton Terrace with a curved road towards the south which was to be named 'Woodleigh'. The proposed houses were designed as large villa residences similar to the style of those which were eventually built on the existing Marine Avenue. This plan however, was abandoned when the railway track was realigned and the present Monkseaton Station was built closer to the village. As a result, Front Street was redesigned and accommodated by shops, along with the present terraced housing forming part of Coronation Crescent, Kenilworth Road and Kensington Gardens.

It is interesting to note that the plan still included 'Holywell Gardens', which when built was in fact named Holywell Avenue, and 'Laurel Avenue' became Queens Road. The street shown as Beech Grove was shortened to become Sanderson Road with Beech Grove eventually being built at a different angle to the rear of Hawthorn Gardens.

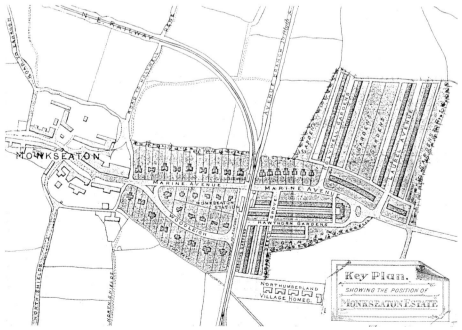

A further plan dated June 1900 was drawn up as the Red House Building Estate with a more intense housing pattern, and also included proposals for a new street layout to the north of the old village street boundary; however this particular design never reached fruition either but some interesting street names are evident on the plan.

33

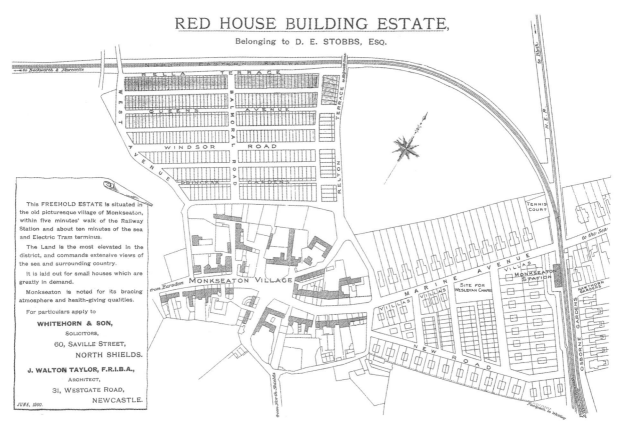

## RED HOUSE BUILDING ESTATE,

Belonging to D. E. STOBBS, Esq.

This FREEHOLD ESTATE is situated in the old picturesque village of Monkseaton, within five minutes' walk of the Railway Station and about ten minutes of the sea and Electric Tram terminus.

The Land is the most elevated in the district, and commands extensive views of the sea and surrounding country.

It is laid out for small houses which are greatly in demand.

Monkseaton is noted for its bracing atmosphere and health-giving qualities.

For particulars apply to

**WHITEHORN & SON,**
SOLICITORS,
60, SAVILLE STREET,
NORTH SHIELDS.

**J. WALTON TAYLOR, F.R.I.B.A.,**
ARCHITECT,
31, WESTGATE ROAD,
NEWCASTLE.

JUNE, 1900.

In later years, proposals for development of the northern section of the lands of Seatonville Farm included the building of Closefield Grove. This land was purchased by Messrs. A. Lisle and Sons. Plans dated November 1939 indicate that Closefield Grove was originally intended to shadow Bromley Avenue for its entire length, as far as Seatonville Road, with further housing development proposed on the area now occupied by 'Bromley Field'.

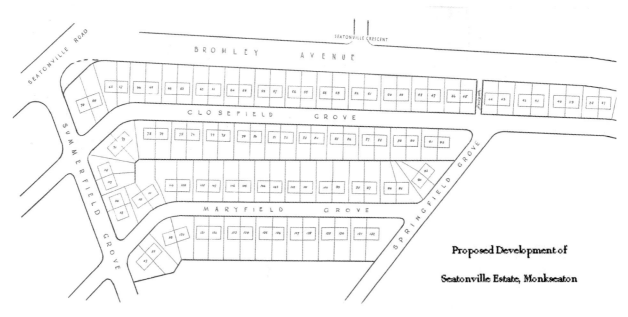

Proposed Development of

Seatonville Estate, Monkseaton

Two street names had been suggested within the plans; 'Maryfield Grove' and 'Summerfield Grove'. This development never fully materialised because the ground on 'Bromley Field' was considered unsuitable due to its marshy and unstable condition. As a result, Closefield Grove ended at the junction with Springfield Grove and 'Bromley Field' was simply left as open recreation land. Many of the other adjacent fields attached to Seatonville Farm were developed during the late 1940s into what became Seatonville Estate, which included the laying out of Pinetree Gardens, Appletree Gardens, Elmtree Gardens and similarly associated streets.

# BYGATE ROAD

It has often been asked why Bygate Road was so named. The most likely explanation is that because prior to the mid 1800s, there were no recognised footpaths in Monkseaton Village. At this time, Front Street was little more than a field path, with a wall and a gate at each end. The nearby divergent road running parallel to the rear of Front Street therefore became known as 'Bye-Gate', and was derived from people passing 'By the Gate', rather than through it. The spelling was later corrupted to 'Bygate', and it is quite probable that at one time, even as a narrow farm-track, Bygate Road was once the main street through Monkseaton. There were two sets of gates on Front Street, one of which was situated at what is now the present junction of Coronation Crescent, and the other at the corner with Chapel Lane. They were removed around 1845, when the road was opened out to become the main route through the village. A well known building that once stood on Bygate Road was called 'Rock Cottage', built in 1790 as part of Bygate Farm. Three Mountain Ash or Rowan trees (sometimes referred to as 'Wychen' trees), stood on Bygate Road, directly outside of Rock Cottage, and separated this house from the main Bygate Farm buildings which stood directly opposite. Much folklore and superstition surrounds this type of tree, as it was

*Looking east on Bygate Road in 1948 showing the three 'Wychen' trees in the middle of the road. Rock Cottage is to the left, with the outbuildings of Bygate Farm to the right.*

believed that they provided protection from malevolent beings, and therefore were originally planted by local farmers in order to ward off evil spirits. In later years when Bygate Road was widened, the trees were left in situ, with the road being built around them, as can be clearly seen in the picture! The trees died off in the 1980s and were eventually replaced with two new saplings – in the middle of the road!

Standing next to Rock Cottage, Lynn Cottage which dates from around 1920 was occupied from 1936 by Christopher P. Scott who was the local chimney sweep. He ran his business from this house and used bicycles as the principal mode of transport. Mr Scott was also the grandson of the proprietor of Scott and Robson's Village Grocery Store which stood next to the Black Horse at the top of Percy Terrace. Travelling further west up Bygate Road, a row of terraced houses dating from the 1800s, and numbered 6, 8 and 10 have unusual wooden porches to the front with symbols on the apex depicting a square and compasses which may have Masonic origins. The reason for this is unknown. Further up the street, beyond the old stone wall is Garden Cottage, which stands near to the corner with Chapel Lane. Built in the 1700s, the cottage is regarded as one of the oldest buildings in Monkseaton, and despite extensive modernisation over the years, it still retains much of its original village charm and character.

*Christopher Scott (foreground) with two unknown employees in front of Lynn Cottage.*

*A 1960s view of Nos. 6, 8 and 10 Bygate Road. These houses each have a wooden porch with Masonic style symbolism on the apex. The reason for this is unknown.*

*Lynn Cottage, Bygate Road, in 1938 The house still stands to this day.*

# CAULDWELL LANE

Cauldwell Lane runs in a north easterly direction from the junction with Earsdon Road into Monkseaton Village. In 1845, it was just a narrow cinder path, the name of which was a spelling corruption taken from the 'Cold Well', which was one of the main water supply sources for the village. The actual well was situated in Town End Close Field, which formed part of the lands of Monkseaton North West Farm (Newsteads) adjacent to Pykerley Road. A second well or spring was also discovered in the adjacent Well Ridge Field, situated slightly west of the Cold Well, and during the droughts of 1868 and 1869, both wells provided sufficient water for the inhabitants of Monkseaton as well as those of nearby Hill Heads, Murton and Earsdon. Interestingly, the quality of the water from each well differed. Whilst the Cold Well water was very soft, the water from the Well Ridge spring was very hard. A separate water supply from the top of Cold Well Lane began with a drain made with flagstones which 'tapped' the gravely sub-soil. Its course followed the path of the present Cauldwell Lane into Monkseaton Village,

*This 1893 sketch by Thomas Eyre Macklin looks west from Front Street towards Cold Well Lane with the edge of the Fold visible towards the right. Rosebery Court now stands here, and where the houses are situated, is where the present shops were built.*

past the front of Percy Terrace to an opening from where the water could be diverted into the reservoirs in the rear garden of Monkseaton House. The water from these reservoirs supplied Monkseaton Brewery next door. When the water supply was not being diverted and allowed to run its natural course, it supplied Nixons' Pond at East Farm (next to the present Ship Inn) which was the usual watering place for cattle and horses. From the top of Cauldwell Lane, there were three drains supplying this water, the first one being situated at the west end of the lane and known as the 'High Drain', the second one was located opposite the end of what is now Bromley Avenue and was known as the 'Middle Drain', and the third one was situated near Percy Terrace and was known as the 'Low Drain'. The water supply has long since disappeared, and has been incorporated within the modern drainage systems as the housing development of the 1920s began. By 1924, housing development was well under way, and Cold Well Lane was widened, to be renamed as Cauldwell Lane, and it was during this time that Oakland Road, Cauldwell Close and Woodleigh Road were laid out. Cauldwell Lane is now a busy main road, feeding Monkseaton Village and Whitley Bay – a distinct difference from the narrow cinder track of over 150 years ago!

*A similar view to T.E. Macklin's sketch looks west towards Cold Well Lane in 1906. The buildings to the right of the picture are 'Murie House' and 'Jessamine House'. (See section on 'The Fold' for details.) Note the sewer gas lamp in the distance, which still stands on the corner of Pykerley Road.*

# CHAPEL LANE

Chapel Lane derived its name from the old stone-built Wesleyan Chapel which stood to the west side of this road, opposite South West Farm stackyard. When the road was

widened during the 1950s, this entailed a partial dismantling of the old stone stackyard wall of South West Farm, which was reduced and rebuilt slightly to the east. By 2005, the land forming part of this stackyard had been sold for development and building work commenced soon afterwards. The site now comprises a small modern housing complex under the name Churchill Court.

*Chapel Lane in the 1950s before widening work.*

## The Chapel

The chapel was built in 1843 by the village grocer, shoemaker, blacksmith and two labourers, and in 1890 some restoration work was carried out, which included the addition of a porch. In 1913, the Wesleyans vacated the premises, but returned for a short while for the duration of the First World War. In 1921, the Chapel was sold to a local dignitary; Col. T.W. Elliott who converted the chapel into a Village Hall, where it was put to general use as a meeting house for the benefit of the local community.
In 1923, an attempt was made to establish Sunday Evening services with lay-preachers, but this was abandoned after nine months because the congregation was small and poorly attended. In 1927, the building was purchased by a Mr Henry B. Saint, a local benefactor, who dedicated it for use by the Congregationalists. He named it; 'Fairway Hall'. A renewed attempt was made to encourage evening services during this year, but

with an average attendance of only 20 these services were also abandoned, however a Sunday School was established in 1928 and proved very popular. Henry Saint was a keen amateur artist and as a member of the North East Coast Art Club, he encouraged a number of local young ladies to paint murals to hang in the premises. In October 1933, eight scenes relating to early Christian history were unveiled and displayed in Fairway Hall for a number of years. During the Second World War, on 29th August 1940, an air raid took place over Monkseaton, and after taking a direct hit with a bomb, the chapel was completely destroyed and never rebuilt. The site was later used as a builder's yard and covered glass store, which eventually became a glazier's workshop. These premises are still evident to this day as Jenkinson's Glaziers.

*Above: Chapel Lane showing the original Chapel to the left, next to which is the village blacksmiths shop and the old 'Three Horse Shoes' Inn. The houses situated behind the tree which still exist to this day, stand towards the end of Chapel Lane close to Front Street.*

*Left: A Sunday School Photograph taken outside the Chapel c.1910.*

## CORONATION ROW

Coronation Row cottages adjoined the old Black Horse Inn and stood on the north side of Front Street, directly opposite the old Methodist Church. Consisting of a total of six single storey residences, the dwellings were originally built in 1821 by Dryden & Co, (the then owners of the nearby Monkseaton Brewery) in order to house brewery workers.

It is highly probable that the cottages derived their name from the coronation of George IV during the same year. The houses were typical of their time, having outside whitewashed walls, stone-flagged floors, with doors and shutters which were painted black within white painted sash frames, and each cottages had its own individual front garden, separated with a small picket fence.

During the 1860s, it is recorded that the middle cottage was called 'Comfy Home', and was occupied by a woman called Sally Smith who was locally known as 'Cat Sally' and famous in the village for her love of cats. She earned a living by making and selling home made sweets, and her little shop was a constant attraction to the village schoolchildren. Apparently her large home-made 'Black Bullets' were renowned, and were a treat which could be bought at a cost of two for a farthing.

Another local character that lived in Coronation Row with his wife; Nanny, was a man called Jack Smith who in his younger days was employed in the ironstone quarries on Whitley Links. During the New Year, he was a favourite 'First-Footer' with all the local farmers with his unvarying toast of; *"May the wing of friendship never lose a feather"*.

A notice in the *Shields Daily News* dated 16th September 1865 advertises an auction to be held at the Commercial Hotel, Howard Street, North Shields at 7pm on Thursday 28th September of that year for the sale of; *'All those six cottages called Coronation-row, situate on the north side of the pleasant village of Monkseaton, aforesaid, let at the annual rental of £25. And all those premises situate behind the above, and comprising two cottages, blacksmith's shop and cartwright's shop and stabling and land suitable for building sites.'*

*Coronation Row in 1910.*

Two of these cottages, along with the old Black Horse Inn, were demolished in 1936, and were replaced with the present public house which now occupies part of the original site. The remaining cottages were converted and used as a shop and showroom by Reg Norie, who for many years established his business as 'Norie' Electrical. (*See Norie Electrical section.*)

Over the years, this building has undergone a number of cosmetic changes, and latterly has been used as business premises for an insurance broker and opticians. Two trees, one of which stands at the front of these premises, and the other in front of the present Black Horse, were originally small saplings, growing in the front gardens of Coronation Row cottages. They have remained untouched here for close to 100 years.

*Workmen commence demolition work on Coronation Row and the Black Horse Inn in 1936. The original garden areas of the cottages can be seen divided by the wooden picket fencing.*

# FRONT STREET

Running through the centre of Monkseaton, Front Street is now the main road through the village; however this wasn't always the case. Prior to the 1800s, Front Street was nothing more than a farm track with a wall and a gate at each end and the nearby divergent road (Bygate Road) became the main route through the village. Opposite the Monkseaton Arms, there were four cottages, which at one time were occupied by men working at Whitley Hill Heads Pit.

All these cottages once had walled front gardens, which disappeared when they were converted to the present shops. A solitary tree still remains and is evidence of the existence of these gardens. It is now surrounded by a low brick wall and probably stood

*Front Street, junction with Coronation Crescent. The wall forming the boundary line of the front gardens of what are now the shops on Front Street is evident in this 1905 photograph.*

within the grounds of either Woodbine Cottage or Clayton House. The four cottages were later converted into the present shops. The gardens of Monkseaton Cottage and Monkseaton House on the opposite side of the street were reduced in size during a road widening scheme in the 1920s, however a 'bulge' in the wall which separates these houses was created to accommodate a large tree which once grew there, indicating the extent of the gardens. Before a numbering system began in the village, most properties were identified by name, and working up the village on the south side of Front Street, the fourth of these cottages was known as 'Woodbine Cottage', which adjoined Clayton House. Clayton House (now No. 21 Front Street) is clearly of Georgian style architecture, however there is evidence to suggest that the rear of the building was originally the front, and once faced onto Bygate Road. When the house was altered in later Victorian years, it was remodelled to face the opposite way onto Front Street. There are records which indicate that Clayton House was also used as a shop which

*Clayton House (21 Front Street) in 1960, with its Victorian style front (left) and Georgian style rear (right).*

40

was owned and run by a Robert Miller, a substantial provision merchant and ship-owner who also owned and built property in North Shields. In 1958, the house was purchased by Mr. C.P. Scott, the son of Christopher and Margaret Scott, who ran the small grocery shop at the top of Percy Terrace from 1905 (Scott & Robson's). The property sale also included Rock Cottage on Bygate Road and a stone Coach-House which

*Looking East on Front Street in 1905. Woodbine Cottage, Clayton House, Gourd Cottage, Lily Cottage, Ivy Cottage and Holly Cottage are evident in the distance. The Black Horse Inn dominates the street to the left.*

once stood in the rear garden of Clayton House. The Coach House was in a poor state of repair and was demolished in the early 1960s. Next door to Clayton House, is Gourd Cottage which is one of the oldest buildings in Monkseaton. There is evidence of an old stone porch at the rear which suggests that at one time like Clayton House, it would also have faced Bygate Road. In 1845, this house was occupied by a Dr Brown who had a practice outside of the village, and in later years was once used as a private school. In 1906 it was taken over by the Quakers and has since become better known as the Friends Meeting House. In 1912, extensive alterations were carried out, especially to the upper floor.

Next door to Gourd Cottage were Lily Cottage, Ivy Cottage and Holly Cottage. All three cottages were advertised to be sold by auction at the Victoria Hotel, Whitley Bay at 7pm on Wednesday, 15th August 1917.

LOT 1. – LILY COTTAGE (Copyhold of the Manor of Tynemouth) Ground Floor: Sitting Room, Kitchen, Bathroom and Scullery. First Floor: 3 Bedrooms. Garden in front, Yard, W.C. and outbuildings in rear. Let to Roger Smith on a monthly tenancy.

LOT 2. – IVY COTTAGE (Copyhold of the Manor of Tynemouth) Ground Floor: 2 Rooms and Scullery. First Floor: 2 Rooms. Garden in front. Let on a weekly tenancy.

LOT 3. HOLLY COTTAGE (Freehold) Ground Floor: 3 Rooms and Scullery. First Floor: 3 Rooms and Bathroom. Garden in front, Yard, W.C. and outbuildings in rear. Let to W.B. Taylor on a quarterly tenancy.

*Lily Cottage (left) and Ivy Cottage (right) in the 1950s*

All of these cottages were demolished in 1961 and replaced by the present Alder Court Flats which were constructed by the local building firm of R.A. Gofton, taking their name from the founder – Richard Alder Gofton. The outbuildings of Village Farm stood next door, occupying the site of the DIY shop, the adjacent buildings and present church. Next door – South West Farm buildings occupied the site of the present supermarket, and crossing the road to the west, the village slaughter house stood on the opposite corner of Chapel Lane and Front Street. Not far from the Black Horse stood a huge whinstone boulder, known as the

'Blue Billy' or 'Big Stone'. This huge stone and the Black Horse corner provided the recognised places for most of the local children to gather and play games, one of which was called 'Boorie' (a kind of marbles). Other games included Football, 'Witty-Witty Way' and 'Shinney' (a type of hockey, played with a cudgel or walking stick). The 'ball' was usually an old cork bung obtained from the nearby Monkseaton Brewery and it was commonplace for many a 'goal' to be scored through one of the windows of the nearby Black Horse Inn.

The 'Blue Billy' was broken up in 1893, and it is said that four cartloads of road metal were obtained from the stone. The open grassed area to the front of the Black Horse Inn (now occupied by a bus shelter and car parking area) was also a place

*When Lily, Ivy and Holly Cottages were demolished, the site was cleared in preparation for the building of Alder Court flats.*

where many of the children in the village gathered to play. Compared to old photographs, Front Street is still easily recognisable, and over the years has changed only cosmetically. The street and all its history still form the central core of Monkseaton Village.

*This 1920s view at the western edge of the village was taken from the front gardens of 'The Fold'. The old Black Horse Inn is in the distance. The houses to the right are Nos. 41 to 51 Front Street.*

# ILFRACOMBE GARDENS

With the arrival of the railway system, Whitley Bay began to expand as a dormitory town and holiday resort, and as such, it was during the early 1900s that Ilfracombe Gardens was laid out to form what could perhaps be considered as the 'boundary' between Monkseaton and Whitley. This street was amongst the first to be built in the early years of the 20th century to accommodate the growing population. Built on land which separated Monkseaton North East (Village) Farm and Whitley Township, a majority of the street was laid out from 1902, with most of the

*Ilfracombe Gardens in 1916. The view looks north from the junction of Marine Avenue.*

remaining work on this and much of the adjacent housing being completed by 1925. Originally an old waggonway connected a number of coal workings at Whitley Lodge where coal was transported to Cullercoats for shipment and burning in the salt pans and limestone quarry at Marden. A large part of Ilfracombe Gardens now runs adjacent to the route of this track which has long since disappeared.

Most of the property on the east side of Ilfracombe Gardens originally consisted of residential terraced housing, and that to the west side were built as shops. The street was once a very significant and important shopping centre, having a well patronised selection of outlets, however over the years as use has changed, some shops have closed down and been converted into flats or houses, and some houses have been converted the other way – into shops. Today, still with a busy trade, Ilfracombe Gardens now connects with the newer Claremont Gardens and Claremont Road to give access to Whitley Lodge Estate.

*Looking south on Ilfracombe Gardens from the junction of Bournemouth Gardens c.1916. The house on the corner is numbered 110, and has since been converted into a shop.*

# MARINE AVENUE

Early ordnance survey maps indicate that Marine Avenue was originally called 'Seaside Lane', and show that it was laid out on land which was originally part of Monkseaton Village Farm (North East Farm). In the mid 1800s, the only system of drainage from Monkseaton Village was an open channel or ditch known as a 'Kundy' which ran alongside the road, which at this time was little more than a narrow pathway.

Before Monkseaton Railway Bridge was built, the road ran on a gentle sloping gradient towards the sea, and waste drainage from the village was set into this channel or 'Kundy' which wound its way down the gradient along the path of Seaside Lane towards the sea, and when development began, a proper underground sewage system was put into place.

*A view looking west on Marine Avenue towards Monkseaton. (Note the individual breaks in the footpath accommodating the driveways into the houses on the right). The signals in the distance mark the level crossing near the old Monkseaton Station. The gable of the large house behind the trees on the left is No. 115 Marine Avenue.*

MARINE AVENUE, MONKSEATON.  (337)

*This view looks east on the Whitley Bay section of Marine Avenue from the junction of Park View and Ilfracombe Gardens. Most of the houses in the distance (numbered 1 to 27) have been converted to become amusement arcades and snack bars and were originally built from 1895 by Nichol Ritchie. After crossing Park Road, the terraced houses then continue up to Nos. 73 (visible on the corner of Park View).*

Building work commenced on Marine Avenue in 1885, and the name of the road changed from that of 'Seaside Lane' to Marine Avenue. The first houses were built by Mr John Potts and Mr James Hilton and were originally called: Carr House, Clifton House, Hazelhurst, Bertlea, Red Lodge, Highfield and The Willows, and in later years when a numbering system was introduced, they became 76 to 88 Marine Avenue respectively. A local society called 'The Monkseaton Village Rooms' produced a report, which in its day aptly described them all as 'Charming Villa Residences'. Over the years that followed, the remainder of the street was gradually built up consisting mostly of large villas, all of which were also given distinctive names.

*Looking west on Marine Avenue towards Monkseaton. Queens Road runs off to the right. The large house on the corner is Rokeby House, followed by Carr House, Clifton House, Hazelhurst, Bertlea and Red Lodge.*

The lower section of Marine Avenue to the east of Ilfracombe Gardens and Park View consists mainly of a row of terraced houses to the south all of which were constructed from 1895 by local builder; Nichol Ritchie. It is difficult to imagine that the buildings which are now filled by amusement arcades and snack bars, occupying the section of Marine Avenue between the Promenade and Park Road, were once family homes. These were the earliest houses, and a terracotta plaque showing this date is evident on the first building of the street. A section of land laid waste at the end of Cliftonville Gardens, accommodates modern flats known as Marine Court East and Marine Court West which were built in the early 1960s.

*Above: A similar view, this time looking east towards Whitley Bay from the junction of Holywell Avenue, showing a different view of the same houses as those shown above. The large house in the distance is called Star Cross, and stands at the junction with Queens Road.*

*Right: A modern photograph of Nos. 125, 127 and 129 Marine Avenue. The end house was No. 129 which stood next to the old railway crossing and was once the residence of the Monkseaton Station master.*

# PERCY TERRACE

Standing in the very heart of Monkseaton Village, it could be argued that one of the oldest streets still remaining is Percy Terrace. This street runs in an easterly direction from the junction of Front Street and Roseberry Terrace, ending at the junction with

Relton Terrace (formerly known as Brewery or Turpin's Lane). Originally, most of the south side of Percy Terrace was taken up by the rear of Monkseaton Brewery and its stable blocks, where much of the old stonework is still evident, all of which at one time formed different parts of the Brewery and outbuildings. The houses and access paths of Nos. 1 to 7 Percy Terrace were laid out slightly above ground level, due to the elevation of the road, and stonework is clearly evident at the base of these buildings. Old ordnance survey maps suggest that these houses were probably built during the 1880s, however it is known that the end building on Percy Terrace which was converted from a shop to a dwelling house in 2004, existed as far back as the early 1800s, and during its lifetime has been a blacksmiths, a grocers, a general dealers and a newsagency.

In 1904, the shop was run as a grocery store by a Christopher and Margaret Scott, who resided next door. At the time, this would have been the main grocery store in Monkseaton Village, which traded under the name of Scott and Robson. As well as selling

*Scott & Robson's grocery store, Percy Terrace c.1910.*

general provisions they also sold a large selection of local farm produce. In 1926, Scott and Robson ceased trading and sold the shop to a George Haimes who took over the business with the addition of a confectioners and newsagency. In 1960, the business came into the hands of A. MacBride, and later to a Mr George Parnaby where it was run as a general dealers and newsagency before its closure and conversion to a

dwelling house. The first Ship Inn stood almost opposite this shop. Originally a farmhouse built in 1688, it was demolished in 1923 to be rebuilt slightly further to the west on its present site. The pub stood next to East Farm, at what is now the junction of Lyndhurst Road, as can be seen in the photo and by the early 1960s the adjacent field and farmland which stood opposite Nos. 1 to 7 Percy Terrace, was sold and laid out to accommodate the present housing.

On 9th July 1927, a stone trough was presented to the Whitley and Monkseaton Urban District Council by the Metropolitan Drinking Fountain and Cattle Trough Association and was erected at the bottom of Percy Terrace, at the junction with Relton Terrace. Much of the inscription on the trough is abbreviated, but is inscribed thus;

*'This trough was presented by the Metropolitan Drinking Fountain Association, and was erected by the Whitley & Monkseaton Urban District Council, at the cost of the local branch of the Northumberland & North Durham Society for the Protection of Animals – July 1927'.*

The trough which still exists, was at one time in regular use by local farm horses and animals, and is now used for ornamental flower displays. The

*This 1930s photograph looks up Percy Terrace and shows the outbuildings of East Farm with the Cattle Trough in the foreground.*

Metropolitan Drinking Fountain and Cattle Trough Association was an association set up in London in 1859 by Samuel Gurney an MP and philanthropist and Edward Thomas Wakefield, a barrister in order to provide free drinking water. Originally called the Metropolitan Free Drinking Fountain Association it changed its name to include cattle troughs in 1867, to also support animal welfare. In collaboration with the Royal Society for the Prevention of Cruelty to Animals, troughs were built for horses, cattle and dogs. The surviving cattle troughs are mainly large granite ones, in many cases planted with flowers. By 1936, the association stopped building troughs, as the automobile was gradually replacing the horse. More drinking fountains were provided in schools and parks, and the old cups were replaced by jets of water as these were seen as more hygienic. The association survives as the Drinking Fountain Association and in 2000 received a National Lottery grant to build more fountains and to restore existing ones. The association now builds drinking fountains in schools, restores existing fountains and provides wells and other water projects in developing countries.

*A 1920s picture taken outside the newly built Ship Inn, at the top of Percy Terrace shows a gathering of cars and motorcycles. The event is unknown.*

# SEATONVILLE ESTATE

Almost all of the present day Seatonville Estate was built on land which originally formed part of Seatonville Farm. As the population of Monkseaton gradually increased, the boundaries of the old village began to expand, and Seatonville Estate was conceived in order to accommodate families in modern Council Housing. Although plans to build the estate were first laid in 1936, building work was deferred due to the outbreak of War. Roads and sewers were laid in 1946, and construction work began in 1947 which also included the laying out of Monkseaton Infants (Appletree Gardens) School. Although much of this housing was built on agricultural land, an area of Common Land known as Chamberlain's Meadow (the first references of which date back to at least 1550) was lost to the development. The project was the area's biggest post-war housing scheme and one which gained high praise as a fine example of modern development with much of the credit being given to Mr A.J. Rousell, the council surveyor, his deputy; Mr Colin Parker and Councillor Mrs F.M. Laws who assisted in the interior layout designs. Special precautions were taken to overcome the effects of possible mining subsidence as old pit workings were evident between 12 and 20 feet underground. The houses were therefore built on concrete 'raft' foundations and it was because of this danger that no terraced houses were built on Seatonville Estate. Nearly all the houses here were semi-detached and consist of a mix of four distinct styles, some having a flat front and gable end or hipped roof, others with a bay window and hipped roof and others based on the style of a bungalow with dormer windows set into the roof.

*Pinetree Gardens, from the Foxhunters junction in 1949.*

The estate itself has an open plan aspect and consists of 14 individual streets, the four primary ones being Pinetree, Appletree, Elmtree and Cedartree Gardens which were developed in an arc around a central triangular grassed area, and with the exception of Churchill and Roker Avenue, these, along with the remaining streets were named in a simple manner after trees, possibly inspired by nearby Maple Avenue most of which had been laid out some years earlier as private housing. Ashtree, Baytree, Birchtree, Cherrytree, Firtree and Oaktree Gardens along with Cedar Close, make up the remainder of the estate, bounded to the south east by Shields Road all of which have a rectangular concrete plaque inset into a wall indicating the name of the individual street. The designs incorporated a row of garages which run parallel to each of the rear lanes at Oaktree Gardens. Another block of prefabricated garages sit to the rear of Cherrytree Gardens along with a grassed recreation area which was cleverly merged into the corner at the rear of Pinetree Gardens and Shields Road. Similarly, another small recreation area to the opposite end of Cherrytree Gardens allows pedestrian access onto Shields Road. Cedar Close which consists of a small loop of terraced bungalows comprising a small covered verandah, was perhaps a good early example of homes which were primarily designed to accommodate elderly persons with ease of access.

*Oaktree Gardens Shops and Flats – 1950.*

The estate was completed in 1951 with the occupancy of the last of its 400 houses and was considered self-sufficient with a variety of shops, all centrally situated in Oaktree Gardens along with a small local rent office which stood in nearby Baytree Gardens. Interestingly, there are no houses or buildings on Ashtree or Birchtree Gardens, which are simply access and exit roads for the estate, and Churchill Avenue is the only street wholly within the estate which does not bear the name of a tree. The reason for this is unknown. The private housing on the eastern side of Roker Avenue which connected Shields Road and Maple Avenue had already been laid out in the late 1920s, so it was logical to retain the name for the remainder of the street when it was built up. The triangular area of grassland between Baytree Gardens and Churchill Avenue was left open as a recreation area, the western edge of which now accommodates Charlton Court Sheltered Housing, and was named as a tribute to a long serving councillor and former Mayor of Whitley Bay during 1959/60 – Roger Mason Charlton. When Seatonville Estate was completed in 1951, work began with the construction of Foxhunters Housing Estate to the opposite side of Shields Road. The houses are of identical design to those on Seatonville Estate, and comprise the streets which make up the southeasten side of Shields Road, ie: Haydon Drive, Bedale Drive, Cotswold Drive and Zetland Drive.

*Looking east on Shields Road in 1954. Birchtree Gardens (Seatonville Estate) runs off to the left, while Haydon Drive (Foxhunters Estate) runs off to the right a little further on.*

# SEATONVILLE ROAD

Old Ordnance Survey Maps indicate that the road connecting Coldwell (Cauldwell) Lane with Rake Lane at Preston Gate was originally known as Turnpike Lane, and later called West Road. Soon after 1928 it became better known as Seatonville Road.

Until the mid 1920s, Seatonville Road was actually a narrow country lane, with two farmhouses situated on it; Burnt House Farm and Seatonville Farm which loaned its name to the road. Over the years, Seatonville Road became the main route to connect Earsdon and Wellfield with the Shields Road from Whitley to Preston and North Shields. Following the demolition of Burnt House Farm in 1929, the road was widened as housing development took place between Cauldwell Lane and Bromley Avenue. This was supplemented with further housing development in 1959 and 1960, following which, nearby Seatonville Farm was demolished.

*This 1920s view shows a narrow Seatonville Road looking south towards the Foxhunters and was taken from the top of Bromley Avenue. Burnt House Farm buildings are to the left and Seatonville Farm is also visible in the distance behind the trees.*

*The block of shops situated at the north end of Seatonville Road was constructed during the mid 1930s. The first businesses that were established there between 1938 to 1940 are listed as follows: No. 1 A.S. Tennant (Chemist). No. 3 No Listing. No. 5 A.R. White (Grocer). No. 7 G.D. Ewen (Butcher). No. 9 M. Hildreth (Fruiterer). No. 11 J. Green. No. 13 A. Harrison (Confectioner). No. 15 F. Anderson (Boot Repairer). No. 19 North Shields Co-operative Society. A & S Tenants' Chemist Shop also incorporated West Monkseaton Post Office, the pillar box of which is visible in the picture.*

In the early 1920s, George Dawson Ewan set up his first butchers shop in Coronation Crescent, Monkseaton. The business was very successful and afforded him the opportunity of expansion by opening a second branch at No. 7 Seatonville Road in 1936. Although the Coronation Crescent shop has long since closed, the shop on Seatonville Road has continued trading from this address. It is still family-owned, and now one of Monkseaton's longest established businesses. Local housing development also began to take shape at the time these shops were built, and as a result, much of the housing situated on the west side of Seatonville Road from Canberra Avenue and Athol Gardens was laid out. This development was advertised as 'West Farm Estate'; however the lands upon which they were built actually formed part of South West Farm. (The lands belonging to West Farm were situated slightly to the west of Cauldwell Avenue.)

*Left: For many years, John Ewan (nephew of the founder – George Dawson Ewen) and one of his longest serving staff members, Vic Homer ran the Seatonville Road shop. This photograph dates to around 1960*

*The Co-operative Store was a well known feature for many years and stood on the corner of Canberra Avenue. The butchery department adjoined the shop around the corner. The premises were taken over by Mills Newsagency and General Dealers in the early*

*1960s, and after some conversion work, the butchery department later became West Monkseaton Post Office.*

# ST RONAN'S ROAD

From its earliest origins, Monkseaton was a small village, surrounded by open fields and consisting of little more than a few farm buildings and dwelling houses. It was not until the late 1800s that much of the expansion and development began as new housing and roads were laid out. St Ronan's Road runs almost parallel to the south side of Front Street following the route of the old footpath which ran through Fancy Field from Whitley into Monkseaton Village. The laying out of this area dates to 1910, which is evident by a terracotta plaque situated on the corner gable of St Ronan's and Kenilworth Road. The architecture in the street indicates that it was designed for retail rather than domestic use, and interestingly, there is no uniformity in the design of the buildings. St Ronan's Road, along with

*Nos. 18, 20 and 22 St Ronan's Road in 1932.*

several adjoining streets appears to have been named with an emphasis on Sir Walter Scott. Three of his novels are entitled; St Ronan's Well, Waverley and Kenilworth, and one of his poems is entitled; Marmion. Scott lived at Abbotsford House and he died at Melrose, so the connection with the similarly named streets in the locality becomes obvious. It is highly probable that the original development of St Ronan's Road was to introduce and accommodate a community of businesses which did not exist in the old part of the village itself. St Ronan's Road once thrived with a variety of shops, and in 1920, Wards directory listed a selection of retail outlets which included four Drapers, two Grocers, two Dairies, two Butchers, two Confectioners, a Hardware Dealer, a Bootmaker, Boot Repairer and Boot Dealer, a Chemist, a Patternmaker, a Post Office, a Newsagent and a Fishmonger. The list is not exhaustive, as over the years many of the businesses changed, however in later years, as new shops became established on the main thoroughfare through Monkseaton, they overshadowed

*In directories dated 1928 and 1930, the listing for C. Taylor's Fishmongers shop was No. 20 St Ronan's Road, however this 1930s photograph clearly shows the premises at No. 22 St Ronan's Road, adjoining No. 1a Melrose Avenue.*

the businesses which were effectively hidden from view on St Ronan's Road, forcing them to close, and today, only a small handful still remain. Some of these shops were eventually converted into houses, and on close inspection, architectural evidence of their existence is still visible today.

Horton's grocery store and Johnson's confectioners stood next door to each other and are listed in directories at Nos. 2 and 4 St Ronan's Road respectively. Extensive alterations have since seen these premises converted into houses, and there is only minimal evidence today of the existence of these shops. Compared to the modern photo shown below, a close inspection of the curved open archway and pilasters adjoining Johnson's shop reveals that it is now the front door of the existing houses re-numbered as Nos. 8a and 8b. Likewise, the pilasters of Horton's shop still remain, and are evident to each side of the present house window.

In 1928, William Horton is recorded as living at No. 2 The Gardens, a house which adjoined his shop to the side. It would appear that he began trading as a Grocer from No. 2 St Ronan's Road in 1911. By 1930, the business ceased and came under the ownership of a T.J. Dobson where it continued at this address into the 1940s. Similarly, Thomas and Dorothy Jane Johnson began trading at No. 4 St. Ronan's Road, around 1911, and after their retirement in 1935, there were no further directory listings for this address or business name.

D.J. Johnson
(Originally 4 St. Ronan's Road)

Horton
(Originally 2 St. Ronan's Road)

# THE FOLD

The Fold is situated within the extent of medieval Monkseaton, which in its present form is still evident today. The name is derived from old English *(Fald)*, and means 'A small enclosure'. In William Weaver Tomlinson's book, *Historical Notes on Cullercoats, Whitley and Monkseaton*, he refers to the area as *'The Fau'd'*. Earliest

records go back to the 1700s, when it is known that the Fold was probably the most industrious part of the village with a saw-pit, a skinnery, a storehouse for wool, a blacksmith, a cooperage, and a village butchers shop. Records also suggest that in 1841, a Mr William Clark ran a school here. A number of old single storey cottages which made up most of the Fold had probably existed from the mid 1600s, with others dating to around 1800. Many of these houses simply consisted of nothing more than a single room with a roof supported by oak lintels

*The Fold c.1890.*

held in place by wooden wedges and chock joints. In 1890, all of the houses and cottages in the Fold came into the possession of a Mr John W. Hutchinson of Tynemouth, but nothing more is known of this. In the early days, these cottages were mainly occupied by tradesmen who were artificers in tin and small crafts and they stood until 1955 when they were eventually demolished for site clearance following air raid damage during the war. Today, the Fold basically comprises a square area of land adjacent to Front Street, with a single row of terraced houses numbered 9 to 19 which

*Joe Davidson, the village blacksmith, had a 'Smithy' to the rear of the Fold.*

are set back from the main road to form its western boundary. The present flats now dominating the Fold were constructed in 1955 following demolition of the old cottages which stood on the site, and the central area was landscaped to form an open aspect. The eastern edge of the Fold backed onto a street called Roseberry Terrace which simply consisted of a short row of houses which were demolished in the early 1960s to make way for the current sheltered housing project, better known as Roseberry Court. Although no

longer recognised as such, Roseberry Terrace still exists, and runs adjacent to the Ship Inn. After the Second World War, the end house of this row, next to Front Street was converted to become Taylor's fish and chip shop, and stood here until it was demolished in the mid 1960s. Roseberry Court, situated on the eastern corner of the Fold, sits on the site of two large stone built houses; 'Murie House' and 'Jessamine House', which were built in 1814, prior to which, the old Seven Stars Inn, dating from the early 1700s, occupied this area. Even in the 1920s, the Fold was still an industrious part of the village, with stables and a blacksmiths shop which were run by a Joe Davidson, and a corner cottage converted to a tyre workshop, run by Mr. A. Young which specialised in puncture repairs, vulcanising and retreading.

This 1925 view of the Fold, at the corner with Front Street, shows the corner cottage, which was converted to accommodate 'The Whitley Bay Tyre Repair Company'. It was replaced with MacGregors Offices, followed by the present 'West House' development.

A similar picture to the one above, shows a row of terraced houses to the right background which still exist. Roseberry Court Sheltered Housing occupies the area of vacant land in the foreground.

On 29th August 1940, a bombing raid occurred over Monkseaton which destroyed a number of houses in the Fold, with nearby property suffering serious damage. As a result, much of the adjacent area was later rebuilt, to include new shops and flats between the Fold and Pykerley Road. In later years a purpose built office block was built to accommodate MacGregor House. When MacGregors vacated the premises, further development in 2004 saw the demolition of this office block which was subsequently replaced with small apartments named West House, named after the large farmhouse belonging to West Farm (also called West House) which stood nearby on the corner of Front Street and Pykerley Road.

The Fold in 1945, showing bomb damage to the rear of Murie and Jessamine House. Note the corrugated Anderson Shelter.

# VERNON DRIVE

Vernon Drive was laid out on a short field track, at the northernmost edge of Monkseaton South Farm and the only road access possible was from Chapel Lane. The first building to be constructed was Monkseaton Senior School which opened in

1932. This was followed in 1938 by two residential houses which were built opposite the school and were later numbered as 2 and 3 Vernon Drive. The road ended where the sharp bend now exists and a wooden fence marked the end of the road, beyond which the open fields of Monkseaton South Farm continued towards Shields Road. Even as later housing on the street developed, Vernon Drive remained as little more than a muddy track but in 1948 a full road surfacing programme, accompanied by the installation of street lighting was planned. The roadworks were later completed at a cost of £3,200 and the North Eastern Electricity Board charged £204 for the installation and supply of lamp posts and lighting. This work coincided with construction of the new Primary School on nearby Appletree Gardens which allowed Vernon Drive to be opened out as a through road to connect with Haig Avenue. The street, which now forms the eastern boundary of the school runs to the rear of Beverley Park

*Wooden posts mark the end of Vernon Drive.*

*Vernon Drive in 1982 showing the extremities of the rear gardens of Beverley Park.*

and remained private until May 1957 when it was finally adopted by the council as a public road. In recent years, six new houses numbered 11 to 17 (with the omission of

No. 13) were built towards the south eastern end of Vernon Drive and were accommodated on land which formed the extremities of the extensive rear gardens of Beverley Park.

*Vernon Drive c.1948. The first houses to be built on this street were Nos. 2 and 3, which are visible to the left.*

# VICTORIA PLACE

Victoria Place is an inconspicuous narrow lane abutted by an old sandstone wall situated next to Lynn Cottage (No. 4 Bygate Road). The lane connects with two old cottages: 'Seaton House' and 'Victoria Cottage' which are enclosed between Bygate Road and Front Street. 'Seaton House' was originally called 'Sea View Cottage' and was once a Victorian Farmhouse (probably part of Village Farm) which has undergone various alterations over the years. Next to it stands 'Victoria Cottage' which was originally a single-storey farm workers dwelling.

*Victoria Place, gives access to Seaton House and Victoria Cottage.*

Both of these properties were offered for sale by public auction at the Victoria Hotel, Whitley Bay on 15th August 1917, and described as follows:

LOT 6 – SEA VIEW COTTAGE *(Now known as Seaton House)*
Ground Floor: Sitting Room, Kitchen and Large Scullery. First Floor: Two Bedrooms and Bathroom (Attic above). Tastefully laid out garden, good greenhouse, poultry run, small summer-house and 3-stalled stable with loft over. This lot is in a secluded position, is of pleasing design and is entered from Bygate Road with a right of way at Front Street. In the occupation of Mrs Phyllis Robinson – Vacant possession on completion.

LOT 7 – VICTORIA COTTAGE:
Adjoining Lot 6.
Ground Floor:
2 Rooms.
First Floor: 2 Rooms.
Garden in Front;
Yard, W.C. and
outbuildings at rear.
Let to Ernest Grice on
a monthly tenancy.

Both lots are
Copyhold of the
Manor of
Tynemouth.

*Victoria Cottage (left) and Seaton House (right).*

# PLACES AND BUILDINGS

## CRAWFORD PARK

Crawford Park comprises a total of 1.77 acres and is an inconspicuous area which is tucked away between Melbourne Crescent and Wembley Avenue with entrances situated on Seatonville Road and Crawford Place, Monkseaton. When the surrounding streets were built up during the 1920s, the park was incorporated and laid out as a small recreational area comprising little more than small lawns, flower beds, two tennis courts and a bowling green. A pavilion which backed onto Melbourne Crescent was designed into the park to provide gardening stores and workspace for the park keeper, as well as toilets, changing rooms, shelter, and facilities for users of the Bowling Green and Tennis Courts. The basic layout of the park has remained almost unchanged since it was built, and is still in regular use, particularly by Whitley and Monkseaton Bowling Club where frequent seasonal tournaments and matches are held. The park and neighbouring street (Crawford Place) was laid out on land which was formerly part of the lands of Monkseaton South West Farm, which in 1813 was under the principal ownership of a Ralph Crawford who was then described as being much respected for his integrity and agricultural knowledge. Although unconfirmed, this may well be the reason for the street and park being so named.

*The almost hidden north east entrance to Crawford Park, as seen from the junction of Melbourne Crescent and Crawford Place.*

## FRANKLAND MOUNT

Frankland Mount is a large house which was built between 1911 and 1912 on a parcel of land within a field forming part of Burnt House Farm. The house still stands to this day, in its own grounds and is now enclosed and almost hidden from view by the surrounding housing of Frankland Drive, Newlands Avenue and Mount Close. Although information is very sparse, it would appear that the house was commissioned by a Herbert Frankland Storey who moved into the property after his marriage to a Barbara Stobbs of Bank Top Farm, Holywell in December 1912. The house is reputed to have been modelled on an identical dwelling in Saskatchewan, Canada where relatives of the couple had lived during the late 1800s. In 1923, the Storeys vacated Frankland Mount and moved south to live in a farm in the New Forest. The house and grounds were subsequently sold and from 1928 to 1930 they are recorded as being in the possession of a Mr W.S. Rolls, an insurance manager. By 1936 Frankland Mount was in the possession of a Mr E. Couzens – a butcher, followed in 1938 by a Mr. W. Nixon, dairyman, which possibly accounts for the outbuildings at the rear of the house which appear to have been tiled out and converted for use as a small dairy. There is also some evidence of stables with overhead hay lofts. Eventually, the property came into the possession of a

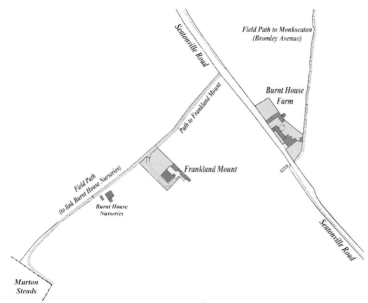

William Wilson Rawes, and later to Oliver Wilson Rawes, who was the Mayor of Whitley Bay from 1968 to 1969. Oliver Rawes was also a prominent local businessman who ran auction rooms and an antique shop on Park View and Whitley Road for many years. By the 1960s, Frankland Mount had fallen into a state of disrepair, and was later sold following his death. In July 2002 the substantial property was sold for £308,000, and the new owners have since carried out extensive repairs, renovations and modernisation work. Access to Frankland Mount was originally gained via a field track running off Seatonville Road, the gateway of which is still evident by the presence of two stone pillars located between Nos. 57 and 59 Seatonville Road. It also allowed access to Burnt House Nursery Gardens, which were developed some years later. The track was situated between what is now the present housing of Athol Gardens and Chatsworth Gardens, eventually narrowing to a pathway which ran adjacent to the south east edge of what became Langley Playing Fields, ending at the boundary fence with Murton Steads Farm. When the present housing development of Newlands Avenue, Mount Close, and Frankland Drive were laid out

*Frankland Mount, 2011.*

in the early 1960s, the track was closed off between Seatonville Road and Newlands Avenue, and the land it occupied was incorporated into the rear gardens of both Athol Gardens and Chatsworth Gardens. Direct access to Frankland Mount was then changed and is now via a private gated driveway running off Frankland Drive.

## GARDEN COTTAGE

Garden Cottage, built from rustic sandstone, stands on Bygate Road near to the corner of Chapel Lane. It was built in the 1700s and ranks as one of the oldest buildings in Monkseaton. In 1845 the house was owned by a Robert Ramsay, a man perhaps regarded as a little eccentric when he commissioned the village blacksmith to manufacture two imitation cannons, which he placed near the roof of this cottage. Although the Napoleonic Wars had long ended, Ramsay believed that should the French ever land and travel along 'Shields Lonnen' (Beverley Road) to invade Monkseaton, then the sight of these cannons would frighten them off! For many years, the imitation artillery earned the cottage the nickname of 'Ramsay's Fort'. Robert

Ramsay earned a living by carrying out any agricultural work that he could locally earn. His own large garden backed onto the stackyard of South West Farm, which he eagerly cultivated with an abundance of herbs, which his wife, Bella would use to manufacture various herbal remedies for all types of illnesses. In fact the villagers of Monkseaton would often come and seek Bella's advice before sending out for the doctor. Over the years, the cottage has been extensively modernised and despite some minor exterior remodelling, it still retains much of its original old-world village charm and character.

*Top left: Garden Cottage in 1930.*

*Bottom left: Compared to the previous image, the only obvious alterations to Garden Cottage in this 1983 picture are to the windows and entrance door.*

# MONKSEATON COTTAGE

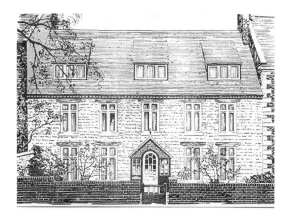

The oldest surviving building in Monkseaton is probably 'Monkseaton Cottage' which stands between the Black Horse Inn and the Monkseaton Arms, on the north side of Front Street. Now numbered as 58 Front Street, records indicate that it was built during the 1400s, possibly as a farm byre, but the passing of subsequent centuries has seen its conversion to the more recognisable dwelling house which exists today. During the late 1800s, it was known to have been the home of a local dignitary; Colonel T.W. Elliott, who was chairman of the Whitley and Monkseaton Urban District Council from 1908 to 1909. Colonel Elliott was related to a John Elliott who owned much of the adjacent property on Front Street and Percy Terrace. He was also a benefactor of the Anglican Church which stood opposite. Before the turn of the 1900s, if village churches were unavailable, it was permissible to hold religious services in private dwellings, and for a short while, and under the auspices of the Church of England, Colonel Elliot provided accommodation at Monkseaton Cottage for church services. Despite the vast age of this house, little else is known of its early origins, and information is fairly scarce.

# MONKSEATON HOUSE

Standing next door to Monkseaton Cottage, and now numbered as 56 Front Street, a keystone above one of the first floor arched windows at the rear of Monkseaton House bears the date 1805, indicating the year it was built. It is recorded that the first occupant was a Dr Roxby and although no other details are known, it is said that for a short time the house was used as a private asylum. In the *Newcastle Courant* dated 28th June 1806, the house was described as; '*A neat new-built mansion house, situated in the healthy and pleasant village of Monkseaton.*' It is recorded that in 1814 and 1816,

*Monkseaton House (right) and Monkseaton Cottage (left) in 1950.*

the house was in the possession of a George Kerr, but by the mid 1800s, had been sold to become the residence of William Davison, the owner of the adjacent Monkseaton Brewery. In order to provide an adequate and plentiful supply of fresh water for the brewery, William Davison had two reservoirs constructed in the rear garden of this house, which were fed from a water channel following the path of nearby Coldwell Lane. The reservoirs have long since been filled in, but it is believed that a tunnel still exists and connects Monkseaton House to the former brewery (now the Monkseaton Arms). To the rear, the house had two stables a laundry and kitchens which were formerly two small cottages. In 1865, the house was sold to a Mr John Elliott who was still shown as the occupant in 1873. It would appear that he also owned the much of the adjacent property, as a report from that year describes his assets as: A Mansion House and Grounds adjoining Monkseaton Brewery on the north side of the village street in his own occupation (Monkseaton House). An eight room dwelling to the west thereof (Monkseaton Cottage). Seven small tiled cottages fronting to the village street, each having one room and two fall pantry but no yard or outbuildings (Coronation Row). A Public House facing up the village (The Black Horse). Seven recently erected two-room houses with enclosed yards and out-offices facing north (Percy Terrace), and a shop with additional room.

A plan dated 1877 no longer show the reservoirs, but instead shows a detailed diagram indicating that Monkseaton Cottage and Monkseaton House shared a huge landscaped rear garden, extending back to Percy Terrace and eastwards behind the brewery buildings to include a Tennis Court, Vinery, Tomato House, Potting Sheds and two small Summer Houses. From the early 1960s these two buildings were merged together to become a residential care home, but have since been converted back to form two separate private properties.

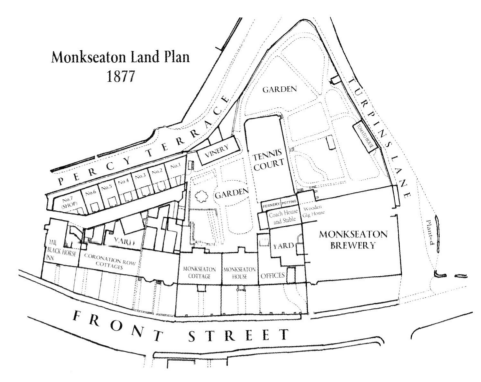

The rear gardens which still extend as far as Percy Terrace to the back, have been substantially reduced in size. In 1953, a new house (numbered 56a Front Street) was built on this land as a surgery for a Dr Ryle and is now a private residence. The eastern part of these gardens now accommodates a block of houses known as Relton Court, next to the Monkseaton Arms. In 2006, Monkseaton House was sold for £500,000.

## THE REGAL CINEMA

Built in Art Deco style, typical of the period, the Regal Cinema occupied a site at the top of Cauldwell Lane. Its imposing frontage curved neatly around the corner into Seatonville Road, where it backed onto Paignton Avenue. Regal Cinema was a limited company formed by three local men; Donald Gilbert, G.H. Bates and H.S. Dixon, along with Edward Hinge who ran a cinema circuit throughout the North East. Designed by Dixon & Bell (Architects), the construction contract was awarded to Thomas Clements of Newcastle. Building work commenced in 1935 and the doors were first opened to the public on 4th November 1936 with the first picture to be shown; *Anything Goes* starring Bing Crosby and Ethel Merman. The managing director was Donald Gilbert, the general manager was George F. Wharton and the resident manager was Joseph Lambert. Admission prices at this time were 1/- for the rear stalls, 9d for the centre stalls and 6d for the front stalls. The cinema building incorporated three adjoining single storey buildings which were situated on Cauldwell Lane. The first occupiers of these buildings were Barclays Bank at No. 155, Eileen Martins Ladies Hairdressing Salon at No. 157, followed by M. Hopkins drapery shop at No. 159.

*The 'Regal' Cinema in 1936. A landmark at West Monkseaton for over 60 years.*

The Regal auditorium had a seating capacity of 1,014 and was a very popular venue for many years, drawing large audiences from all over the area. Children's Saturday matinees and performances also proved to be an extremely popular attraction.

In July 1949, ownership of the Regal transferred to Essoldo Cinemas, however the established name was retained. By the early 1960s, television audiences had probably cut into the market causing a significant decline in attendance figures, and so on 11th August 1964, the cinema closed with its final film, *The Longest Day*. Thereafter, the building became a bingo hall for a period of just over seven years. By the early 1970s, public demand once again changed, and so the building underwent extensive renovations and internal modernisation work including a full refit. It reopened as the 'Classic' Cinema on 2nd April 1972 showing its first film: *Waterloo*, starring Rod Steiger. In July 1977, further alteration

# THE REGAL
MONKSEATON

Managing Director - - - - - DONALD GILBERT
General Manager - - - - GEORGE F. WHARTON
Resident Manager - - - - - JOSEPH LAMBERT

Prices of Admission:
REAR STALLS - 1/- (including Tax).
CENTRE STALLS 9d. do.
FRONT STALLS 6d.

Continuous from 6 p.m.
Doors open 5.30 p.m.

Matinees : Wednesday and Saturday
at 2.15 p.m.

Prices: 4d., 6d., 9d., (inc. Tax)

Car Park adjoining Cinema or Cauldwell Lane

Regal Cinema
Monkseaton

December, 1937

CONTINUOUS FROM 6 P.M.
DOORS OPEN 5-30 P.M.

Playhouse
Whitley Bay

REGAL BINGO Monkseaton
Open EVERY Night
Commencing at 7.30 p.m. prompt
(Pensioners Half Price Monday and Thursday)
SUNDAYS, MONDAYS, THURSDAYS
& SATURDAYS ........ Admission 2/-, Books 2/-
FRIDAYS ...................... Admission 2/-, Books 2/6
SEVENTH HOUSE ................. £68 on 47 numbers
Every Saturday night £10 Free House given away
CLOSED TUESDAYS

*The grand old building with its landmark corner frontage faced a sad ending in August 2000 when it was demolished and replaced with studio style housing apartments.*

work took place to convert it to a twin-screen theatre, which later operated under the name of the 'Cannon'. With the advent of modern out of town multiplex theatres, and declining audiences, the cinema which had once again been renamed, this time as the 'ABC', closed its doors for the last time on 15th April 1999.

# ROCK COTTAGE

'Rock Cottage' was a well known building that once stood on Bygate Road, and was originally built in 1790 as part of Bygate Farm. In 1821, it is known that a John and Ann Dunn resided in this house and was evident by an inscription carved into a stone block above the front doorway which bore their initials:

D
J     A
1821

This stone was often referred to as a Wedding Stone, which for many years was pointed out to tourists during the life of the cottage. A coach-house and stable once stood behind Rock Cottage, which was used in the mid 1800s by the village carrier, Robert Duxfield who was affectionately known as 'Bob Dyuk'. Following his death, a William Ackinclose (known as 'Willie Akkum', took over the premises to continue the business of village carrier. It is recorded that during the winter of 1886, a great snowstorm swept over Monkseaton, and during the night, a huge drift piled up against the front of Rock Cottage, completely covering the bedroom windows. By 1965, Rock Cottage was under the ownership of a Christopher Scott, a native of Monkseaton who demolished the cottage because of its poor state of repair. The old Wedding Stone was removed from above the door, and placed in the rear garden of Clayton House (21 Front Street, Monkseaton). A new house called 'Rockville Bungalow' now stands on the site of Rock Cottage. Land to the side of this bungalow, on Coronation Crescent was at one time occupied by nursery gardens which were removed in 1960. The area is now used as a car park.

*Above: The 'Wedding Stone' bearing the initials of John and Ann Dunn.*

*Left: Rock Cottage was demolished in 1965. The 'Wedding Stone' is still visible above the door.*

## SOUTER PARK

When the old Monkseaton Station was demolished in 1915, the North Eastern Railway Company held title to the land, which was still lying derelict in 1921. It was during this year that a deputation of Whitley ratepayers called on Whitley Council to develop the site, and so discussions were held by the Council to purchase the land for the laying out of a recreational park. Councillor C.W. Souter, whose residence was adjacent to the site of the old station at No. 7 Osborne Gardens, led negotiations with the North Eastern Railway Company, and was instrumental in acquiring the site on behalf of Whitley Council. Despite some opposition to the cost, the unemployment grants committee agreed to allow the Council to borrow £3,900 in order to utilise unemployed labour to assist in laying out the new park on both the north and south side of Marine Avenue which was to include Putting Greens, Bowling Greens, Tennis Courts and landscaping to provide for flower beds. The park was completed in November 1922, and Councillor Souter's efforts were recognised when the park was named in his honour, as a result of which, he provided

*2011 – In the foreground is the only remaining evidence of the fountain donated by Councillor Souter in 1923.*

63

an ornamental drinking fountain which was installed in the park in May 1923 and stood there for many years. In December 1946, a statue surmounting the fountain was stolen and never recovered. Souter Park has been in continual use since it was opened, and still exists to this day with many of its original facilities.

The Whitley and Monkseaton Bowling Club has been established at Souter Park since 1924 when it was formed by several members of nearby Monkseaton Methodist Church. Membership was originally restricted to men only, however a Ladies Bowling Club was formed shortly afterwards and those games were played on an adjacent green. In 2006, both clubs were amalgamated. The first club president was Councillor Souter who held this post for 20 years. Perhaps the most famous member of the club was Syd Drysdale, who captained the winning England bowling team at the 1962 Commonwealth Games. Membership of the club gradually increased and was eventually limited to 160, however there is no longer any restriction on membership numbers, and anyone who has an interest is welcome to contact the club. Souter Park and the bowling greens are maintained by North Tyneside Council, which are open from April to September each year. The club play in various leagues each week and comprise men's, ladies and mixed games. There are various club competitions which run during the season and the club is very active and well supported.

*Souter Park Bowling Green in 1930.*

*Right and below: Whitley and Monkseaton Bowling Club, Souter Park in the 1940s.*

# THE VILLAGE HOMES

In 1868, James Hall, a wealthy Tynemouth Shipowner was instrumental in setting up the *Wellesley* Training Ship in North Shields. The vessel was intended to act as an industrial school, preparing homeless and destitute boys who were unconvicted of crime for a life at sea, and by 1877, he decided to turn his attention to girls in a similar plight. It was during this year that he felt that there was a need to create an institution for the reception and training of little girls who were either orphaned or destitute, and called for subscribers to come forward to establish a home where the training would work on the family principle of; *'Instruction in household duties which are strictly such as a woman would have to discharge in a poor man's home'*.

Wellesley Training Ship, North Shields

It was proposed that girls would be admitted between the ages of 6 and 12 years, and would normally leave on attaining the age of 16 years. In 1879, the Duke of Northumberland provided a site between Norham Road and Duchess Street, with construction costs being met by a number of local wealthy benefactors, and so the Northumberland Village Homes for Homeless and Destitute Girls was formed. (It is interesting to note that the nearby streets – Percy Avenue, Alnwick Avenue, Warkworth Avenue, Countess Avenue, Duke Street and Duchess Street are appropriately named, having obvious links to the Duke of Northumberland.) Building work commenced on the Village Homes the same year and the first block of cottages was opened in 1880. Several others were subsequently added by the generosity of various donors viz: Nos. 2 & 3 in 1882 and 1883, No. 4 in 1884 and No. 5 in 1888. A schoolroom was added in 1883, a lodge and laundry in 1891 and a final extension was completed in 1908. Each cottage had its own 'Matron' or 'Mother', and the entire complex was occupied by a maximum of 150 girls, many of whom were brought in, in rags and tatters, and were kitted out in the homes distinctive uniform of a blue serge dress and a red cape. The institution was licensed as an industrial school and its aim was as follows: *'To provide reception and training of little girls being orphaned or destitute or found wandering without home or settled place of abode, proper guardianship or visible means of subsistence'*. By the 1970s the homes were no longer in use, and they eventually closed in 1986, when the site was taken over for development to a modern housing project.

Although now extensively modernised, all of the original cottages still remain and have been tastefully integrated with newer buildings and selectively landscaped to accommodate individual and modern private housing needs. The site is now known as Village Court.

*Left: The Village Homes in 1910. The house in the foreground is now number 96 Village Court.*

# TRADE AND BUSINESS
## GOFTON'S

The Gofton family have had roots in Monkseaton since at least 1877, and their history goes back through more than five generations. Although some early details are sketchy, 1881 census records indicate that a Richard Alder Gofton was residing in Eleanor Street, Cullercoats having the occupation of a joiner, and this appears to be the first indication of any connection with the building trade. Richard died in 1891 at the age of 94 years. Other records indicate that a Richard Gofton was a soldier who served with the Coldstream Guards and saw active service during the Boer War. Various members of the Gofton family were also

*This photograph showing the workforce of Gofton Bros. is believed to date to around the 1930s. It is unclear exactly where the photograph was taken, but likely that it was close to one of their many residences in the area of Uplands, Monkseaton. Members of the Gofton family are indicated as follows: Back row, 10th from left: D. Gofton. Second row, 6th from left: L. Gofton. Front row (standing), 1st and 2nd from left: J. Gofton and A. Gofton.*

bell-ringers and had a long association with St Paul's Church at Whitley Bay as well as other local churches in the area. Thomas Thompson Gofton is recorded as the Ringing Master at St Paul's Belfry, Whitley Bay and his death is recorded on 3rd June 1931 aged 59 years.

The locally established name of Gofton Brothers has long been associated with Monkseaton. After the First World War, the Gofton Brothers had become well established as building contractors, joiners, cabinet makers and undertakers, and over the years were well documented in local directories at various addresses in the area, many of which it will be noted were in the Hillcrest area of Monkseaton from the late 1920s. Richard Alder Gofton Jnr was born in 1903, and William Longworth Gofton was born in 1905 and by 1935, they became members of Brier Dene Lodge at Whitley Bay, where they were both actively involved in Freemasonry for many years. In 1949, South West Farm buildings, which were situated on the corner of Front Street and Chapel Lane in Monkseaton were no longer in use and as such the main farm outbuildings

*High profile advertising.*

which included the old stables and cow byres backing onto Front Street were taken over by Gofton Bros. Extensive alteration work was carried out, as the premises were converted to accommodate a new showroom for sanitary ware, fireplaces, interior household fittings and building materials etc. and incorporated a joinery workshop. The premises were completely restyled and named: 'Corner House', trading under the name of R.A. Gofton, with the catchphrase: 'The Showrooms with a Garden'. This was particularly evident during the 1950s with a magnificent ornamental garden being situated in front of the showroom which included a miniature stream with a pond and bridge, dressed with rockeries and flower beds. The premises opened for business in March 1950, and closed down after about 10 years successful trading, but sadly the colourful gardens were lost to accommodate a car parking area.

*Gofton's – 'The Showrooms with a Garden'.*

Gofton Bros. were responsible for much of the building work in the area, particularly during the 1930s when they constructed many houses in the Monkseaton streets which bear a single name, ie: Hillcrest, Uplands, Hillfield, Hazeldene, Hermiston, Ivanhoe, Denebank and Deneholm, as well as those to the south of the Monkseaton/West Monkseaton section of the railway line: Highbury, Holmlands and Ashbrooke.

Other prominent building contracts which Gofton Bros. carried out in Monkseaton over the years included: St Peter's Church, Elmwood Road (1937), South West Farm conversion (1949), Alder Court, Front Street (1960s) and Wilson's Car Showroom, Front Street/Bromley Avenue (1960s).

*South West Farm, Monkseaton in 1948.*

*Gofton's begin alteration and renovation work on South West Farm in 1949.*

*Building work is complete by March 1950.*

*A change of use to a local convenience store, 2010.*

# DEAKIN PRINTERS

An announcement in the *Whitley Seaside Chronicle* dated 4th July 1947 states that 'Deakin Printing Services' of Monkseaton will undergo a change of ownership to become known as Deakin (Printers) Limited. There is speculation that the company first operated with some basic printing machinery from a small workshop somewhere in Monkseaton Village during the mid 1940s before becoming established at No. 33 Front Street (the former Village Farmhouse situated next to the Methodist Church).

During the 1950s to the very early 1960s, these premises were shared with Tyne Taxis who operated from a small room on the ground floor. It is known that two of the early partners of the company were Jim and Arthur McAndrew, however no records exist of the firm's early origins, or indeed why it was actually called 'Deakin'. As the company developed, up to three Heidelberg Platen printing presses were

*Kelly's Shop and Deakin Printers in 1984. The small 'Island' in front of the building once housed a petrol pump. (See Monkseaton Garage section.)*

installed which were capable of printing in black and white as well as single colours and much of the early work involved the production of posters and leaflets etc. Most of the typesetting and proof-reading took place on the upper floor. A fire occurred at the premises in April 1982 which caused over £30,000 worth of damage to stock and machinery, however the firm quickly recovered and in 1984, Deakin took over the long established firm of J.H. Brown (Printers) of York Road, Whitley Bay, to eventually incorporate the business within the main print shop in Monkseaton. Deakin Printers operated from 33 Front Street for a period of 40 years before their growth dictated a necessary move, and in December 1987 new and larger premises were secured on Earsdon Road at West Monkseaton. Deakin Printers are now one of the oldest and longest established businesses in Monkseaton and they continue to flourish. With the introduction of new state of the art machinery, digital print processing and print finishing facilities the company are capable of producing in-house, everything from basic single colour leaflets to full colour booklets and brochures. From its simple origins in the 1940s, the success story continues with over 18 employees.

# H.W. HUNTER

*A familiar sight in Monkseaton, as one of Hunter's buses crosses Monkseaton Railway Bridge.*

Although not directly involved with the history of Monkseaton, Hunter's distinctive dark brown and cream buses were a familiar sight for many years as they travelled their route through the village. H.W. Hunter operated from Westbourne Garage on Westbourne Terrace, Seaton Delaval and commenced operations in 1929 when three second hand vehicles were purchased from another Northumberland operator (Lee of Rothbury). Their first open-back Double Deckers (registration numbers DJR 681 and ETY 912) were a pair of Leyland PD2's which arrived in 1950 and 1951 and survived to provide regular service until the 1970s. During 1971, their third double-decker arrived which was a modern Leyland Atlantean, registration number WTY 841J followed in later years by a number of other vehicles to supplement their fleet. Interestingly, and unlike some of the other large operators in the area, Hunter's buses never actively displayed any commercial advertisements on their vehicles. The main bus operator in the area for many years was United Automobile Services; however H.W. Hunter was only a small private operator who ran an intermediate service from Seaton Delaval to North Shields via Earsdon, Monkseaton, Whitley Bay and Preston Village, usually terminating at Northumberland Square. This was a route not covered by United.

Part of Hunter's bus route would occasionally overlap sections which were run by the United service, particularly through Monkseaton into Whitley Bay, and where this happened, many regular travellers preferred to wait an extra few minutes for Hunters to arrive rather than travel by the red United service. As well as running a service route, Hunter's also had a small fleet of coaches which were available for private hire.

By 1964 the business was being run by J.K. Hunter, trading as H.W. Hunter and Sons. The business changed hands in the early 1970s becoming a limited company under the name H.W. Hunter and Sons (Seaton Delaval) Ltd. In later years many changes were made to bus services including deregulation and a standardised numbering system was introduced. As a result, Hunter's service which previously had no service number was allocated service No. 810, and their route was extended as far as Seghill and Cramlington. The company ceased trading on 26th July 1994, and Westbourne Garage was sold.

# FOXHUNTERS TRADING ESTATE

The Foxhunters Trading Estate was developed in the 1950s, and became home to a number of local businesses. Perhaps the most famous of all of these was the 'Coast Creamery' whose distinctive red logo adorned many of the milk bottles delivered to thousands of homes throughout the area particularly during the 1960s. At the time, the dairy and bottling plant was one of the most modern of its type in the country. In this 1970s aerial photograph, the creamery dominated much of the estate, and can be seen to the centre left of the roadway, with the transport depot almost opposite. Shields Road is just off camera at the bottom of the picture and Foxhunters Road runs up the centre into the estate with part of Marden Farm Estate visible in the upper background. Working down the photograph, the main established businesses on the estate included;
1. W. Bush (Plant Hire.
2. James White (Brick Depot).

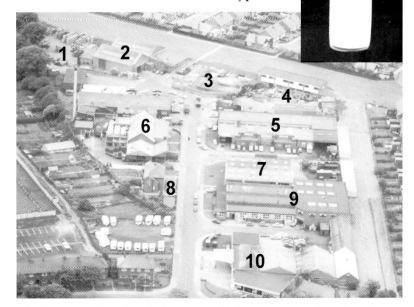

3. North Eastern Electricity Board (Storage Yard). 4. Greenwell & Guy Temple (Road Maintenance & Builders). 5. Robertsons (Bakery & Distribution Depot). 6 & 7. Coast Creamery (Dairy & Milk Bottling). 8. Coast Creamery Maintenance Manager's House. 9. Marc Curtis (Clothing Manufacturer). 10. Foxhunters Garage. (Petrol Station & Garage Services). Other interesting features show the allotment gardens and a caravan storage area which stood adjacent to Whitley Bay Football Ground. The car parking area to the rear of Shields Road still exists today. As many of the manufacturing firms moved on or ceased trading, a majority of the estate has now been taken up by a number of used car sales outlets. Of all the original and established businesses on this estate, only Bush Plant Hire remains.

# MACGREGOR'S

Brothers, Robert and Joseph MacGregor were engineers who lived in Monkseaton Village. Their experience in the field of Naval Architecture had taught them much, and in 1929, they patented a revolutionary design for the steel hatch cover. In order to promote, sell and develop this idea, the brothers formed MacGregor & Company in 1937. The brothers were aware that if ships were to operate economically, they must not waste time in port handling cargo inefficiently, so their simple design consisted of five articulated leaves that stowed neatly at the end of each hatch. The Second World War also proved the value of watertight steel hatch covers as a means of keeping badly damaged ships afloat. In 1945 the MacGregor brothers teamed up with Mr Henri Kummerman, the result of which was a rapid increase in the use of the covers and a growing appreciation of the economic advantages. The three men

*Joseph MacGregor in 1949.*

concerned went on to form a world wide organisation to promote devices, not only for safety, but for the efficient operating of ships.

*MacGregor House and the Fold in 1967.*

*For many years, the well known MacGregor Logo consisted of a ship fronted by a depiction of a hatch cover.*

The first company design office and headquarters was constructed in Monkseaton in 1957, at the corner of Front Street, on the site of the old Fold cottages which had been demolished a year earlier. Their main workshop and factory which produced the covers was situated in neighbouring Blyth, which also included a development unit.

MacGregor's remained in Monkseaton for 47 years until 2004, when larger out of town premises were sought. MacGregor House was demolished soon afterwards to make way for a new apartment block called West House. Today, the MacGregor Group is now part of the Cargotec Corporation, the global market leader in engineering and service solutions for the maritime transportation and offshore industries. Ship owners, ship and port operators and shipyards in the commercial marine and offshore industries are their customers. Products include hatch covers, cranes, equipment for RoRo ships and ports, and solutions for cargo lashing, bulk handling, offshore load-handling and naval logistics. From very humble beginnings in Monkseaton, MacGregor's 2007 net sales totalled 748 million Euros.

At the end of December 2007, the company employed a total of 2,223 people, and now operates in 50 major shipping and shipbuilding centres throughout the world.

# JENKINSON GLAZIERS

John Jenkinson (popularly known locally as 'Jackie') established the firm of Jenkinson Glaziers just after returning home from active service in India at the end of the Second World War. Jackie learned his trade when he served his apprenticeship as a Leaded Window Light maker with Elders Walker in Newcastle during the late 1940s. Using the skills he acquired as an apprentice, Jack together with his brother Colin, rented property at the rear of Princes Gardens, Monkseaton and bought all the necessary equipment in order to produce stained glass, leaded lights and window panes.

These early beginnings soon firmly established their business. As the demand and trend for leaded windows grew, business quickly increased, as a result of which, Jack and Colin manufactured and supplied many of the leaded windows for a majority of the houses which were built in Whitley Bay, and the surrounding areas between 1946 and the mid 1950s. A fine example of a leaded glass window, depicting Diana the huntress, which was designed and manufactured during the 1950s by Jenkinson's, is still evident on an upstairs window at No. 25 Canberra Avenue, West Monkseaton, which for a time was their residence.

*Prospect House, Marine Avenue.*

Some years ago and inspired by this scene, the then owners of Prospect House (125 Marine Avenue, Monkseaton) commissioned a similar window, once again depicting Diana the Huntress to be installed to the ground floor side sash windows of the property.

As the company flourished and continued to expand, Jenkinson Glaziers moved to larger premises in Chapel Lane during the early 1960s where it is still based. These premises, stand on the site of the old Methodist Chapel which was bombed during a wartime air raid in 1940.

Colin Jenkinson was a keen motorcyclist, who often travelled to jobs on his bike, and before such a high emphasis was put on road safety, Colin was often seen carrying his tools and even sheets of glass with him. Sadly he died tragically in the 1950s as a result of a motorcycle accident.

*Jenkinson's workshop, Chapel Lane in 1974.*

Some years later, during the 1990s Jackie also died, as a result of which the business eventually came out of family ownership; however it still operates to this day as one of Monkseaton's longest established businesses.

*Jackie and Colin Jenkinson outside their premises which are situated between the rear of Nos. 7 and 9 Princes Gardens in 1952. The vehicle, registration number HBB288 was a Morris 10 van. (Princes Gardens was formerly known as Princess Gardens – hence the apparent incorrect spelling of the street name on the side of the van.)*

*Fireshield Extinguisher Services now occupy these premises, where Marc Rutherford and Chris Bradley are happy to pose for a modern 2011 equivalent photograph.*

# MONKSEATON BANKS

As banking technology has progressed with an increased usage of Credit Cards, Debit Cards, ATM machines and latterly the internet, the need for a physical banking service in Monkseaton has now diminished. Many of the former well known and established banks which once formed a major part of the daily business in the village have gradually disappeared over the years. Since the 1920s five banks were recorded within the Monkseaton area, and are listed as follows:

*Lloyds Bank, Monkseaton in 1982.*

1. Barclays: 42 Earsdon Road, opened during the 1960s and closure in the 1990s when it afterwards became West Monkseaton Post Office.

2. National Provincial Bank (later to become National Westminster or NatWest): 42 Cauldwell Lane, which existed from the 1960s to the 1990s.

3. The Trustee Savings Bank (TSB) stood on the corner of Front Street and Pykerley Road from the 1950s until closure in the early 1990s.

4. Lloyds was the newest and most recent bank which stood between Monkseaton House and the Monkseaton Arms at No. 54 Front Street, from the 1960s to the late 1990s. This was a modern purpose built detached single storey building and was the last bank in Monkseaton to close.

5. The oldest and longest established bank in Monkseaton, however, was Martin's Bank, situated at No. 24 Front Street which existed from about 1927 to the 1970s.

# MONKSEATON GARAGE

In 1914, a James Turton of Monkseaton purchased an area of land between Front Street and Bygate Road, which was formerly occupied by the grounds of Monkseaton Village Farm. In 1916, he built a large house on part of the site which is now evident as No. 12 Bygate Road. Hidden away behind Monkseaton Methodist Church, one of the larger outbuildings of the farm became Monkseaton Garage, which Turton established soon after the end of World War One. Although most of the remaining stone farm outbuildings still stand, they now have commercial and storage uses for nearby businesses.

Monkseaton Garage existed for a number of years, and was used as a service and repair centre, with the present DIY shop (built in the early 1930s) being used as a car showroom for a short while. Fuel was dispensed from a pump which stood on the small 'island' next to the church (adjacent to Front Street), which has been latterly used as the site for a community notice board. Eventually, the business and house at 12 Bygate Road was inherited by Mr Tom Shields, the grandson of James Turton. In 1946, Tom Shields expanded on his grandfather's garage business and also established a small company within the garage premises which he named 'Pioneer Mixers'. This company manufactured cement mixers for the construction industry where many thousands of them were bought by customers in the UK, with others being exported abroad, particularly to South Africa. 'Pioneer Mixers' ran successfully until 1971 when demand declined. Production at the premises eventually ceased and the garage business also closed. The garage was later taken over and subsequent usage has included offices, motor servicing and storage facilities for a car hire company.

*Monkseaton Garage c.1932. James Turton is in the centre of the picture wearing a trilby hat and to the right is a staff member, Billy Williams.*

## OUTRAM'S GARAGE

Wards 1930 directory, shows William Outram residing at No. 85 Cauldwell Lane, Monkseaton. Little is known of the Outram family; however in 1926 William Outram established and built a service station known as South Grange Garage on Earsdon Road, West Monkseaton which continued under this name into the 1940s. The actual building was based on a South American design which Outram brought back from Brazil during the early 1920s. Prominently situated on the west side of Earsdon Road, at the junction with Cauldwell Avenue, the external appearance of the building has barely changed, and in later years became better known simply as 'Outram's Garage'.

Since the business was established, it has provided all the usual facilities associated with a garage including a personal forecourt service and petrol pumps. As a family owned business, the 1950s and 1960s saw the business appointed as a Rootes Group dealership, selling a small range of new cars. In later years, the advent of larger service stations with cut price fuel meant that smaller garages such as

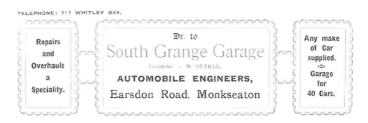

*Am invoice header from the early 1930s. The claim that there were facilities to garage 40 cars at these premises may be somewhat exaggerated.*

Outram's were unable to compete, and as a result the forecourt services were withdrawn during the 1970s leaving the garage to concentrate on Motor Repairs, servicing and M.O.T. Testing. By the 1980s the business had changed hands and although it continues to retain the established and well respected name, it is no longer in Outram's family ownership. The garage still thrives as an independent concern offering a full range of automotive services as well as used car sales facilities.

# NORIE ELECTRICAL

Coronation Row Cottages stood immediately to the east of the old Black Horse Inn. Many of these cottages were demolished when the Black Horse Inn was rebuilt in 1936, however, one of the cottages remained and was used as an office and workshop that was later to become familiar as Norie Electrical. Reg Norie Senior established the business in 1908, which in 1945 was renamed Norie's Electrical Construction Company. It was around this time that a bow window frontage was added to the cottage to convert it into a little shop that many people will remember. During the mid 1960s, the building was demolished and completely rebuilt as a modern shop, numbered 64 Front Street, and carefully styled to remain in keeping with the pattern of the previous building. It was named 'Grid House'. Over the years, the business thrived in Monkseaton, and was well stocked with a vast selection of electrical goods and general hardware. As the shop was so centrally situated in the village, part of the premises were converted into a coffee shop for a time, and it became a popular venue for a morning chat, a hot drink and a bite to eat! The large house next door – No. 66 Front Street, was for a time owned by Reg Norie Junior, and later converted to accommodate a launderette to compliment the business. Combined with the growth of out of town shops and discount stores, the business fell into a short decline so Reg Norie took this opportunity to retire, and the business finally ceased trading in 1984.

*Reg Norie's Electrical Shop in the 1930s.*

*Norie's Electrical Shop under demolition in the 1960s. The premises were replaced by a modern building which still stands today.*

The premises were taken over by R. Monckton-Milnes and Partners and the premises were re-named; 'Collingham House'. Monckton-Milnes were then a well established firm of Independent Financial Advisors and Insurance Brokers, founded in 1964 by Mr Robert Monckton-Milnes of Darlington, and first operated from a practice in Park Avenue, Whitley Bay. The company had a portfolio of over 10,000 clients, both individual and corporate, covering a world wide geographic range. Over the years, 64 Front Street has undergone a number of cosmetic changes, and latterly became the business premises for N. Robinsons Optometrists.

*Conversion work begins on the new shop in the 1960s.*

*Nories familiar trademark and logo which was used in nearly all of their advertising material.*

# TAYLOR'S GARAGE

The history of Taylor's Garage is really the history of the Taylor family, and in particular of Mr John Beaumont Taylor, who was the founder of the company and also a most remarkable man. One of the few who foresaw the pace of expansion with regard to the motor car, John Taylor began his working life in engineering, in the Elswick Gun Sight Shops of Armstrong-Whitworths at Newcastle. From there, he graduated to Marine Engineering and travelled the world until returning to the North East to become a jig and tool designer on field guns and tank guns during the First World War, once again with Armstrong-Whitworths. The war had brought tremendous strides forward in motoring, and so in May 1920, Mr Taylor opened for business as a motor car and motor cycle repairer, trading under the name 'The Monkseaton Motor and Repair Works'. To accommodate the business, a wooden building was erected on a field fronting Earsdon Road, Monkseaton, which at this time was a narrow country road with hedges and ditches on both sides. The building measured 100 feet by 20 feet, and the only other buildings standing between the Foxhunters roundabout and West Monkseaton Station were Seatonville Farm, Burnt House Farm, and Monkseaton Grange Farm, all of which have now long since disappeared. The 1920s were of course hard times,

*Mr. John Beaumont Taylor, founder.*

but Taylor's were quickly becoming known as a forward-thinking organisation, and in 1922 had installed the first roadside petrol pump on the North East coast. By 1927, they had a total of eleven petrol pumps selling petrol at 11d per gallon (or if you preferred the more expensive grade, 1/- per gallon)! In 1930, Mr John Cowell Hodgson became a partner with the firm. Previously a schoolmaster at Backworth School he became a good friend of the Taylor family during the hard and difficult times of the early 1930s and was greatly missed when he died in 1937. The transition from The Monkseaton Motor and Repair Works to its subsequent development of what became Taylor's Garage was particularly notable in the 1930s. In 1932, the wooden building was demolished, and a new garage was built, complete with a hydraulic lift, Tecalemit greasing bay and much of the modern equipment

*Development of the Rotary Engine takes place in Taylor's Workshop, Earsdon Road c.1938.*

that was available at the time. In 1933, this led to Taylor's being appointed by Vauxhall Motors as the main Vauxhall dealership for the area. John Taylor still continued his interest in engineering and in 1934 became involved in the development of a multi-cylindered rotary engine with Jack Edmundson of Jesmond Garage, another enthusiast. This engine gave great promise of future development. They made complete drawings and Mr Taylor built a machine shop extension on the garage at Earsdon Road in order to build this experimental engine. During the next five years they worked relentlessly on the engine. It was revolutionary in its day having no axis torque, but maintaining the same power and speed in either direction. The engine attracted attention from many well-known engineering firms including Parsons Marine Turbine Co. However if the end of the First World War indirectly aided the expansion of Taylor's, the advent of the Second World War meant that the engineering projects had to be shelved. From the outbreak of the war, the machine shop was used to manufacture tools, gun parts and hydraulic gear for battleships etc. They also trained many girls in fitting and machining for the larger factories. Despite rationing, the end of hostilities marked the return of normal motor and repair work, and in 1949 the son of the founder, Mr John H.B. Taylor had joined the firm. Steady progress was maintained and in 1955 a new showroom and parts facilities were added to the Earsdon Road premises. Two years later, Vauxhall

Motors upgraded Taylor's to Vauxhall-Bedford Main Dealers status, which meant that they could deal direct with the factory for all their products. Never content to stand still, in 1958 the parts department was once more extended, actually doubling its size. By 1959, due to the growth of the company, additional premises were acquired in Park Road and Marine Gardens, Whitley Bay, which allowed sufficient room to accommodate an extra large showroom, service

*John Beaumont Taylor's small wooden garage stood on Earsdon Road, and established as the 'Monkseaton Motor and Repair Works'.*

departments, plus paint and body shops. Up to 1969, there were constant improvements, and the installation of up to date equipment ensured that customers received the best possible service, not only for new cars, but also in the after sales and used car areas. It was during 1969 that the latest in a line of Taylor's, namely John Wentworth Taylor, a grandson of the founder started with the firm. Since John Beaumont Taylor founded the business in 1920, it became part of the fabric of the area, and Taylor's can be justly proud of the part they have played in it. The business ceased in 1985 when it sold out to Reg Vardy's Car Dealership.

TAYLORS GARAGE For EXPERT CAR REPAIRING

Complete Overhauls
Cylinder Reboring
Electrical Repairs
Acetylene Welding
Cellulose Body Spraying

Tecalemit High Pressure Greasing
High Pressure Washing
Battery Charging and Repairs
Radiator Repairs, etc. etc.

ANY MAKE OF NEW CAR SUPPLIED.
Exchanges and Deferred Terms Arranged.

VAUXHALL SPECIALISTS
Officially appointed " A.A " and " R.A.C. "

TAYLORS GARAGE

(Monkseaton) Ltd.
EARSDON ROAD
MONKSEATON       'Phone 321.

*A 1930s newspaper advertisement.*

*Fronting Earsdon Road in 1929, this view shows some of the first-ever roadside petrol pumps that were installed at the Earsdon Road premises in 1922. The houses near the end of Grange Park can be seen in the background, along with Grange Farm, which stood on the site of the present Hunting Lodge Pub.*

The front section of the garage premises were later demolished to make way for a modern petrol filling station, and later, a car wash with the remaining buildings being converted to small trade outlets.

*Taylor's Garage, Earsdon Road in 1958. The 'Grange' Hotel sits in the background.*

## REEVES

Reeves timber and hardware store was a well established business in Monkseaton Village. The shop was situated next to Lily, Holly and Ivy Cottages (now Alder Court). The following edited extract, written by Colin Reeves (son of the founder) gives some personal recollections, memories and interesting facts about one of Monkseaton's oldest businesses.

'Before migrating to Australia in 1965, I lived in Whitley Bay for 20 years. My father owned a timber and hardware business (now Kelly's Hardware), situated at 31 Front Street, Monkseaton. He began his business at 33 Front Street which was set well back from the street. The ground floor was occupied by Tyne Taxis, and to the rear; Deakin Printers. My dad occupied the top two rooms. As a young lad, I was enchanted by this building. The top floor was approached by ascending a steep stairway, and at the top, customers would pause on a narrow width of decking. A metre in front it dropped three steps into a narrow passageway and down there was a magical space to explore. One standout memory that seemed to encapsulate No. 33 Front Street was a very large painting on the far wall of the room to the right at the top of the stairs which depicted a rural scene. During my boyhood days, I recall the dip down from Monkseaton Station Bridge then through a bank of shops before rising up to No. 31 Front Street whereupon I disappeared into a bygone past with one foot in the present.

I recall Tyne Taxis well. The drivers wore brown uniforms with peaked caps askew on their heads. As for the taxis, they too were brown. There was an interesting character by the name of Jim Spoors (in his 70th year during the 1960s) who would hang out at Tyne Taxis as well as working part-time for my father. I think his second home could well have been the Black Horse!

My father was very compassionate and altruistic. He was always ready to give freely as well as helping people who through no fault of their own were down on their luck, lost or afflicted in some way. His motto was – 'There but for the grace of God'.

I cannot be specific as to when my father first set up his business at 33 Front Street but I can reasonably guess that it was shortly after the war. In the 1950s and 1960s, at the back of 31 Front Street, there were three outbuildings made from roughly hewn stone. I believe these were once stables. My father rented a couple for timber storage and a workshop. In one of them was a partitioning wall that fell short of the roof. On the top, tucked between the stonework I once found a Napoleonic coin. Unfortunately, soon after my discovery I lost it. The single storey building attached to No. 33 also gave up some secrets. My father and one of his employees (most likely his right-hand man, Tom Kelly who eventually bought the business), when up inside the roof came across two substantial copper kettles and a stringless lute. On it, there were many indentations suggesting perhaps that it had been imbedded with precious stones. The latter relic, though somewhat ruinous was greatly treasured by my father.

I can still remember being a pupil of Bygate Infant School, but in short, Monkseaton has left me with many indelible memories'.

Reeves Timber and Hardware was sold to Tom Kelly in 1967 and underwent a name change to reflect its new ownership. The business thrived and after 36 years, Tom retired in 2003 after selling out to one of his employees. The shop remains in its original location at 31 Front Street, in the heart of Monkseaton and after continuous trading for over 65 years, it remains as one of the oldest and longest established businesses in the village.

# TYNE TAXIS

Tyne Taxis were a substantial company which originated in Newcastle. The main office and garages were located at Dinsdale Place, Shieldfield and they had a smaller 'branch office' in Gateshead with the other one being situated at 33 Front Street, Monkseaton. This office was nothing more than a room which was once shared with Deakin Printers, in the former Village Farmhouse. Their early fleet of three Austin FX3 diesel cabs were painted in a very distinguishing khaki brown colour and were well known throughout the area. The drivers even wore a brown uniform with a matching peaked cap. Perhaps the most well known of these drivers was a character called Percy Harding, who was often nicknamed 'Humpy Percy', a loyal and long serving driver with Tyne Taxis for many years. Percy was given this unfortunate name because of his pronounced stoop and rounded back.

The Tyne Taxis fleet of brown FX3 cabs was eventually replaced in the 1960s with three modern black Austin Cambridge saloon cars all of which were serviced from their main premises in Dinsdale Place, Newcastle. The call-taker and dispatcher at the Monkseaton office for many years was a Bob Storey who lived in Cullercoats. The foreman and lead driver was a Sid Cartwright and apart from Percy Harding, the other driver was Ronnie Jenkinson of Wellfield. Their advertising was always very simple and basic. An illustrated pictorial advertisement in the *Whitley Bay Guardian and Seaside Chronicle* dated 8th July 1949 stated nothing more than: 'Take a Tyne Taxi – Ring Whitley Bay 2200'. Even by 1957, the advertising tag-line remained unchanged. The only difference was an alteration to the telephone number which was now shown as Whitley Bay 22200, and in 1975, a half page advert in the local telephone directory remained exactly the same; 'Take a Tyne Taxi'. The Monkseaton branch of Tyne Taxis was bought out in 1975 by Mr Doug Boyd and taken under the wing of his company; A1 Taxis which was situated on Park Avenue, Whitley Bay. The Monkseaton office was subsequently closed following the takeover.

*A 1975 advertisement.*

# WEST MONKSEATON OPEN CAST

After the Second World War, the country was saddled with huge debts, food was in short supply and rationing was still in force, however the potential earnings from coal were exploited by the government to assist in meeting these debts. In February 1948, the first coal was removed from a site on Rake Lane, and by the summer of the same year, open cast mining work commenced at West Monkseaton on the area adjacent to the new station and railway line (formerly part of Monkseaton North West Farm – Newsteads). The contractors at Rake Lane were Holloway Bros. and those at West Monkseaton were Sir Lindsay Parkinson. The Rake Lane site was short lived and restored in 1949, however the terrific upheaval at West

*A Monighan 6-W dragline (left) and a Lima 1201 (right) at work on the West Monkseaton site in 1950.*

Monkseaton became a prominent feature of the local landscape which lasted 5 years and affected many housing development plans around the area. For a short while, the huge spoil heaps around the site earned it the nickname of 'The Monkseaton Alps'.

*The landscape scars are evident in this 1949 view of West Monkseaton open cast site. Thorntree Drive, Melville Gardens, Marina Drive and part of Sandringham Drive (visible to the top centre of the picture) are still under construction and the small rectangular area of land adjacent to Earsdon Road which comprises part of Newsteads Farm remains intact. The Railway line runs diagonally from the left towards West Monkseaton Station where it passes under Earsdon Road bridge. The houses to the lower left corner comprise Uplands and Hillfield.*

*Spoil Heaps, adjacent to West Monkseaton Station.*

*The usually white frontage of West Monkseaton Station is caked in coal dust during the mining operations.*

*Reclamation work begins adjacent to West Monkseaton Station in late 1953.*

Heavy machinery and earth-moving equipment could be heard night and day and was sometimes enlivened by the occasional sound of explosives. Water and mud enveloped much of the site, and on dry or windy days, the entire area was shrouded in clouds of swirling choking grey dust which settled everywhere. Earsdon Road was left intact, and the 120 foot deep site which comprised a large area of land, stretched from the rear of Newsteads Farm buildings on Earsdon Road towards Uplands, extending north beyond the present Monkseaton Drive and Golf Course and as far west as Wellfield. Many residents in Uplands suffered flooding to their houses and rear gardens, and it took years for the National Coal Board to settle the resulting compensation claims.

Millions of tons of coal were won here and after five years mining, the site became exhausted and finally closed down in June 1953 to allow for reclamation of the land, much to the relief of the residents. A short string of allotment gardens were then created next to West Monkseaton Station, and eventually the remaining land was allocated for building purposes, where part of Red House Farm Estate and the present supermarket are currently situated.

# WILSON'S GARAGE

During the early 1920s, William Skillbeck conducted business as a Motor Garage proprietor in Annfield Plain, Co. Durham. By 1925 as his business had expanded, he acquired premises at No. 506 Whitley Road, Whitley Bay. (This section of Whitley Road was later renamed Park View.) The premises became a Motor Garage and Showroom, and were situated between the junctions of Marine Avenue and Marine Gardens. The garage comprised a car and motorcycle showroom with a workshop above, and a single petrol pump located on the front footpath just outside the main entrance. Cars for repair were taken to the rear of the premises, where they were transported to the upper floor by means of an electric lift, which was situated in the back lane next to Marine Gardens. The right side of the showroom was used for new cars, and the left for new motorcycles. Two of the first employees at this garage were a Mr Bob Toovey and a Mr W. Popham. During the First World War, Bob Toovey was the works manager of the famous NUT Motor Cycle Works, in Newcastle. At this time the owner, William Skillbeck employed a Mr Robert Wilson, a native of Whitley Bay who was well experienced in the motor trade, to take full charge of the Park View premises when they opened for business in April 1925. The garage quickly became a success, and were soon appointed as agents for Austin, Morris, MG and Wolseley cars.

William Skillbeck eventually sold the business to Robert Wilson, who went into partnership with Bob Toovey. The partnership however failed, and Bob Toovey eventually left. Despite this, Robert Wilson continued with his efforts, and over the years that followed, the business continued to flourish, and it became necessary to employ extra staff. The growth of the business convinced Robert Wilson to make it a limited company, and so the preparations were made. The directors were appointed as Mr & Mrs Robert Wilson, Mr Wilson's nephew, Mr McCaw, and a Mr Raine. The business was renamed R. Wilson Ltd, and so the company was born. Expansion meant that new premises were required, and in 1929, a new purpose built garage was erected at the corner of Cauldwell Lane and Bromley Avenue, which became R. Wilson (Monkseaton) Ltd. The premises at Park View continued to be used as a showroom for new and second-hand cars until 1936, when it was sold, and the entire business was transferred to the Monkseaton premises. Soon after opening, the demand for work was so high that the Monkseaton garage provided an all night service for customers. One of the first employees that worked at the Whitley Bay garage in

*A copy of a 1938 sales invoice for supplying a brand new Morris 10/4 saloon motor car, with part exchange allowance to a Mr Spears, of Monkseaton.*

*Wilson's Garage in the early 1960s.*

1925 was Mr W. Popham, then aged 17. He remained with the company from that time until 1943, when he was rewarded with the post of assistant manager. Soon afterwards, he was promoted to the position of general manager. He eventually retired from the company in 1952 after a total of 27 years faithful service. By 1942, Robert Wilson decided to sell the business, and soon afterwards, it was successfully purchased by a group of four brothers; Norman, Wilf, Harold and Reg Craven. In later years, another member of the family; Derek Craven joined the business as a salesman and was later promoted to the position of Managing Director. Because of the high reputation that Robert Wilson had earned over the years, the Craven Brothers decided that the name of the company should remain unchanged and therefore retained the well-established name of R. Wilson Ltd. Harold Craven

*Wilson's Service Van c.1964.*

became chairman of the company, outlived his brothers and died in the early 1980s when management of the company was passed on to Mr Jeff Stewart who had been with the company for many years.

During the Second World War, Wilson's Garage was under contract with the Ministry of Supply, to overhaul Army vehicles and it was also used as a local base for the Auxiliary Fire Service which housed at least one fire engine and tender. The main garage premises in Monkseaton suffered blast damage, during an Air Raid in 1942.

During the mid 1950s, a site was acquired on the corner of Cauldwell Lane and Woodleigh Road (*below*) to develop as their showroom and after sales facilities, however by the early 1960s the site had outlived its usefulness and a plot of land was purchased opposite the main garage on the corner of Front Street and Bromley Avenue, where a purpose built two-storey showroom was erected, and opened in 1967.

The now defunct showroom at the corner of Woodleigh Road was slightly altered, and taken over to become Monkseaton Library. Just opposite the old showroom on Cauldwell Lane, next to the main garage building, a small shop was acquired, and served as a parts and accessories department for the garage. During earlier expansion of the company, the Craven brothers acquired the Collingwood Garage at Billy Mill. This was followed with the purchase of the Coast Road Motor Company situated on the corner of Queen Alexandra Road and Hawkeys Lane, North Shields. Collingwood Garage was later sold, however ownership of the Coast Road Motor Company remained with the Craven Brothers until 1993 when this part of the business was also sold. Later expansion allowed Wilson's to operate a body shop and accident repair centre on Norham Road, North Shields that complimented the turnover and size of their long established business in Monkseaton, which at its peak employed over 40 people. From Robert Wilson's earliest days in 1925, the business have been dealers for many of the major British Car manufacturers, including Austin, Morris, MG, Wolseley, Riley, Daimler, Jaguar, Lanchester, Triumph and Rover. During the 1970s, British Leyland went through a difficult period and business in the motor trade declined as major manufacturers encouraged large glass-fronted out of town dealerships rather than smaller in-town showrooms. This took its toll on the 77 year old business which began to suffer and was forced to close in 2002.

The garage site and showroom were later replaced with controversial apartment blocks. Wilson's Garage dominated the junction of Cauldwell Lane and Bromley Avenue. When the garage was first built in 1929, it was regarded as one of the most modern and up to date of its time, and the style of the building along with its corrugated asbestos roof typically depicts this. The business offered an extensive workshop covering a full range of servicing and repairs, along with an attended sheltered forecourt facility for the sale of petrol and oil. During the mid 1980s, a countrywide boom in self-service stations with modern and more convenient drive in facilities along with discounted fuel prices meant that many smaller garages went out of business. Wilson's of course was no different, and the forecourt facility closed in 1985. The space however was not lost – it was converted to accommodate the storage of used cars offered for sale.

*This picture taken during the early 1950s shows the small group of houses that stood on the corner of Front Street and Bromley Avenue, prior to the new car showroom being built. Collectively, the houses were known as 'Bromley Place'.*

*When Bromley Place was demolished, the land lay derelict until Wilson's new showroom was built in the mid 1960s. This view was taken from the same location as the above picture.*

*Above: The size of Wilson's Garage becomes apparent in this 1982 photograph, with the showroom in the distance, the main garage in the centre and the parts shop to the right. Note the petrol pump facilities.*

*Right: The Management Team of Wilson's Garage, c.1967 posing beside the company's Bull-Nose Morris Cowley. From left to right: Mr Derek Craven (Managing Director), Mr George Carr (Sales Manager), Mr Harold Craven (Chairman) and Mr Bert Moss.*

# INNS AND TAVERNS

## THE BEACON

On 9th May 1955, planning approval was granted to allow for the building of a new public house on the west side of Earsdon Road at West Monkseaton. Construction work began in 1957 and the premises opened for business under the name of 'The Beacon Hotel' later that year. The name was considered appropriate because the beacon of St Mary's Lighthouse to the east was clearly visible across the then open fields which stood opposite the pub. Over the years, the pub has undergone a number of alterations both internally and externally. Major refurbishment work in March 1998 contributed to an increase in size of almost 50% from its original 1950s layout.

## THE BLACK HORSE INN

The Black Horse Inn which was built in 1793 stood on the north side of Monkseaton Front Street. The building was originally a two-storey stone structure which was remodelled some years later to include a third floor, and almost dominated this part of Front Street. For many years during its life, it was used as a public meeting place, the earliest example of which was indicated in the *Newcastle Courant* dated 1798 in an article which read: *'At Gawen Watson's sign of the Black Horse, a meeting of the creditors of Timothy Duxfield will be held on the Twenty Fourth day of September 1798'.* An old document dated 1815 describes the premises in possession of a Peregrine Henzell; an innkeeper of Newcastle, and Reay Johnson Archbold, late of Morpeth, and were described as: *'A messuage or dwelling house, used as a Public House, with a yard and a garden behind the same.'* In 1827 and 1828, the proprietor is recorded as a Thomas Yellowley, followed in 1834 and 1841 by a John Duxfield, and in 1845 by a Henry Whitfield. Records indicate that by 1855 the Black Horse was actually closed as a public house however it still retained a licence to sell ales and spirits. It was occupied at this time by a George Davidson, a local blacksmith and cartwright when it was used as a venue for winter assemblies which sometimes involved dancing until the early hours. A notice in the *Shields Daily News* dated 16th September 1865 advertises an auction to be held at the Commercial Hotel, Howard Street, North Shields at 7pm on Thursday 28th September of that year for the sale of: *'All that very commodious road-side inn, known by the sign of the 'Black Horse', situate in the village of Monkseaton, as in the occupation of Jane Dawson, a yearly tenant; annual rental, £15'.* Beyond that, in 1869, the premises were sold to a John Elliott, and by 1887 were being run by a Joseph Bell. In 1897, the landlord is recorded as a William Hills, who died in 1908, but strangely enough, was still recorded as the licensee in 1910.

*This painting by an unknown artist shows the Black Horse Inn around the mid 1800s. The original Ship Inn is visible to the extreme left, with Monkseaton Brewery Chimney in the distance.*

*The original 3-storey Black Horse Inn 1904.*

The Inn thereafter came under the ownership of Robinson and Anderson, a company who applied to the Whitley and Monkseaton Urban District Council to demolish and then rebuild the premises to a new design on the same site. This application was approved in March 1936, and demolition work began almost immediately to include some of the adjacent cottages situated next door on Coronation Row. The Black Horse was immediately rebuilt on the same site to its present familiar design and still stands to this day.

*The Black Horse is a fine building, the exterior of which has remained virtually unchanged since it was rebuilt in 1937. However, some minor alterations which are evident include the removal of the bow window and side entrance door which was once the 'bottle and jug' off sales area. This was replaced with a flat window to accommodate a larger interior lounge area.*

*The main entrance door and frontage was slightly modified when alterations to the bar area resulted in the front door being offset to the left and replaced by a second window. This 1961 photograph shows the pub prior to that alteration work.*

## THE GRANGE HOTEL

By the mid 1930s, West Monkseaton had experienced rapid housing development, prior to which it was an area surrounded by fields with only the main road to Newcastle passing through it. Today it is a densely populated residential area with a metro station at its centre. As the area grew, the needs of the residents were met with a small shopping centre on nearby Seatonville Road, a modern cinema, and a new public house – The Grange Hotel which opened on Wednesday 16th July 1937. Built in art deco style typical of the period, the Grange Hotel was an impressive building which was constructed on the site of Monkseaton Grange Farm by Messrs Elliot Bros of Otterburn Terrace, Jesmond. The architect was a Mr. J.R. Wallace of North Shields. A press article in the *Whitley Seaside Chronicle* dated 18th July 1937 colourfully describes the building as follows: 'The Grange Hotel is an impressive building situated on the Earsdon Road. Only 200 yards south of West Monkseaton Station and will rank as one of the finest hotels in the country. The Main entrance is on the Earsdon Road facing east and there are also entrances on all sides of the building, while at the back there is a spacious car park with accommodation for over one hundred cars. On the ground floor there is a large bar and buffet, a public lounge 24ft x 16ft and a smoke room 22ft x 16ft. At the back is a further lounge 22ft x 34ft with French windows facing onto the car park. In the lounges and smoke room are service counters, splendid fireplaces and clocks in all departments. The furnishings are smart, futuristic and pleasing. On the first floor, arrived at by a large staircase, there is a staircase hall, an assembly room 22ft x 35ft, facing east and west; a public luncheon room 22ft x 24ft, two large bedrooms, manager's room and bathroom, and on the final floor are further bedrooms. The decorative scheme throughout the building is artistic, light and bright. This first class hotel is owned by The Northumberland Hotels Ltd. A fine modern range in the hotel kitchen is supplied by the well known firm of Messrs Henry Walker & Co Ltd of Newcastle who have also supplied all the hardware required and the general comfort of patrons has been the foremost thought of the proprietors'.

Although there are entrance doorways to both the north and south side of the building, the main entrance was through the front four-pillar portico, which also included a fine example of curved glass windows to the central section, which enclosed what was once the shop or 'off-sales' area. Of all the managers over the years, perhaps the most popular and well known of these was Mr Alfie Tonks who ran the pub during the 1950s and early 1960s. Although the pub has undergone no external alterations of significance, a major refurbishment in 1962 also brought with it a meaningless change of name to 'The Hunting Lodge'.

# THE MONKSEATON ARMS & BREWERY

According to legend, ale was brewed in Monkseaton, and sold to travellers in the days when the Prior of Tynemouth owned lands in the village. By 1683, the need for a brewery was recognised and so Monkseaton Brewery was built for a Michael Turpin of Murton. Standing on the north side of Front Street, it was the largest and most conspicuous building in the area. It had whitewashed walls, a red pantiled roof and a tall chimney, with corbel heads on the north and south gables. The building could be seen for many miles around. Horse-drawn drays would be loaded with barrels of ale, at the side of the brewery through a 'Loading Hole' which was a kind of dock formed so that the barrels could be run directly off the ground onto the cart or dray. Farmers

Adams Series. Old Monkseaton Village. 284.

delivering cartloads of barley to the brewery would wait at the side of the building next to the grain spouts, and along with the draymen were usually rewarded with a 'Horn' of ale before leaving. During this time, Michael Turpin bought a cottage, which adjoined the brewery buildings and was used as the brewery offices. Many years later, the offices were converted to become the original 'Monkseaton Arms', first recorded and mentioned in 1876, when it was run by a Mrs Mary Ann Wood. Trade directories show subsequent landlords of the Monkseaton Arms as follows: 1887; Thos. Forster, 1890; Roger Rickerton Smith, 1894; William Hill, 1901; William Canfield, 1906; William Young and 1910; William J. Costello. Michael Turpin loaned his name to the road that ran alongside the brewery and through the fields towards Red House Farm, ie: 'Turpin's Lane'. The road was sometimes referred to as Brewery Lane, until the present day housing appeared when it was renamed as Relton Terrace. The Brewery and cottage were sold in 1692 to a George Johnson, later passing to a William Johnson, who died in 1752. The *Newcastle Journal*, dated 28th April 1753 advertises the cottage to be let, and described as; *'Consisting of a good kitchen, 2 parlours, both wainscoted, 3 chambers, one hung with green harrateen (a kind of stuff or cloth), the others with paper, 2 large light closets, and a ceil'd garret, a garden and a large back yard with good water, a good stable and malting'*. Subsequent owners and tenants of the brewery are recorded as; 1787; William Dunn, 1792; Robert Clayton, 1803; Benjamin Brunton, 1804; Samuel

Hurry, 1821; William Davison, 1827; Thomas Dryden & Co. (Ale & Porter Brewers), 1841; Edward Sinclair & Co.

Three fires are also recorded at the brewery, the first of which occurred on 9th March 1821, totally destroying the drying kiln along with 60 bolls of malt. The second fire occurred on 4th January 1849 when the malting and stables were burned down. Five of the six brewery horses perished, and were buried in Chamberlain's Meadow. The third fire occurred in 1860, destroying part of the buildings containing

*The sheer size and scale of the brewery buildings are evident on this sketch by an unknown artist.*

much of the brewery machinery, however all of the damage was repaired. In 1850, there were about 30 or 40 ale-houses in the neighbourhood that were tied to the brewery to supply their ale and porter. In 1855, the Brewery was still under the ownership of William Davison who resided at Monkseaton House, to the west of the brewery buildings. Two reservoirs were built in the rear garden of this house in order to supply the brewery with water. Above the stables and in premises on the opposite side of Turpin's Lane, maltmaking was carried out. The ale, after cooling on the upper brewery floors, was tunned into barrels on gauntries standing in rows on the cellar floors. (The fermentation took place in the barrels.) The yeast would overflow out of the bung-holes and drip into the gauntries, where it was gathered up and placed into a large tub standing just inside the main building, and after being sufficiently diluted with water and whisked around with a heather besom, the dipper was hung over the edge and it was ready for sale.

A notice in the *Shields Daily News* dated 16th September 1865 advertises an auction to be held at the Commercial Hotel, Howard Street, North Shields at 7pm on Thursday 28th September of that year for the sale of: 'All that spacious and substantial building known as MONKSEATON BREWERY, together with the offices, managers residence, extensive stabling, coopers shop, cart shed, malt kiln &c., connected therewith, situate on the north side of the village of Monkseaton, near North Shields. This important property is well adapted for the carrying on of a profitable business. In its past history the vend of beer &c., brewed on the premises has been very large. By an enterprising business man the eligible opportunity now offered of acquiring such desirable business premises, so advantageously situated at a sufficient distance from the town of North Shields to be exempt from its rates, yet sufficiently near to participate in all its advantages should not be overlooked. This property is also capable of being converted into a spacious hotel and family lodging house, and its extent, position and proximity to both the railway station and Whitley Sands would warrant the outlay necessary for such a purpose, and ensure a speedy and remunerative return'.

A further set of sale particulars show that the brewery property was to be auctioned on 22nd October 1866, only

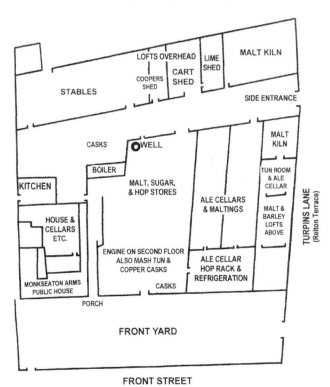

*Plan of Monkseaton Brewery, 1879.*

a year following the previous sale notice. The sale was to be held at the Queens Head Inn, Pilgrim Street, Newcastle, and referred to the premises as follows: 'Offices, managers residence, extensive stabling, coopers shop, cart shed, malt kilns and fixed plant, together with right of user of the water in the ponds on the adjoining property belonging to Mr John Elliott, and of conveying water through pipes, as agreed on 16th January 1865. The brewery is capable of brewing 55 half barrels and the plant is of the best description, and combines the latest improvements. A retail spirit licence is attached to the premises. The brewery is close to Whitley Station on the Blyth and Tyne Railway'.

The brewery was purchased and came into the possession of David Matthews & Son, who had an excellent reputation for brewing the finest Ales and Porter. Twenty years later, in 1886, the brewery was once again advertised for sale by public auction on the premises, particulars of which read: 'All that copyhold brewery and malting premises, with fully licensed public house attached at Monkseaton, and known as the Monkseaton Brewery, together with the brewery machinery, plant and rolling stock, consisting of about 300 casks, spring vans etc. etc. There is an abundant supply of good

brewing water connected with the property. These premises are modern and well arranged on the gravitation principle, and are situate within a few hundred yards of the Monkseaton Station on the adjoining North Eastern Railway (Newcastle and Tynemouth Branch).' The property was sold that day to a George Wright, a brewer of Belford.

By 1900, the brewery and public house had been taken over by the Northumberland Brewery Company, and in 1934 were sold to Newcastle Breweries. Shortly afterwards, the entire site was demolished and the present Monkseaton Arms was built.

A small stone building, situated between the old Monkseaton Arms and Monkseaton House, was formerly used as a harness-room for the brewery, and when the brewery was demolished this building remained and was taken over and run as a pet shop for a number of years by an M. Blackbourn. It was demolished in February 1962 to make

*Since this picture of the Monkseaton Arms was taken in 1982, various alterations have taken place including the addition of a large conservatory which now occupies most of the former car parking area.*

way for a small branch of Lloyds Bank, and later converted into a shop. Part of the old brewery still remains, and consists of a section of the old stone wall, which formed the back of the premises and is evident to the rear of the present Monkseaton Arms. Other stonework from the brewery has been used in the construction of boundary walls for nearby residential premises. Today, the Monkseaton Arms is affectionately known to the regulars as 'The Monkey', and two of the longest serving managers at these premises in recent times were; Kathy Barton and Ken Driver.

Belle Vue House, which adjoins the Monkseaton Arms on Relton Terrace, was preserved following demolition of the old brewery building.

# THE RAILWAY INN

The history and origins of the Railway Inn at Whitley Hill Heads go back many years and begin prior to 1815 with the Crown and Thistle public house which once stood on Hill Heads Road close to what is now the present junction of Dowling Avenue.

Because of its close proximity to the old waggonway, the Crown and Thistle was locally nicknamed as 'The Railway', and in later years was later physically renamed as such. In the early 1900s, the manager was a John Dawson, and the accompanying picture shows him and his wife; Esther standing at the doorway under the signboard.

*The Rose and Thistle, Hill Heads. Later renamed as The Railway Inn.*

The inn closed and was demolished in 1927, to make way for the present housing which forms the southern section of Hill Heads Estate (ie. between Kingsley and Sycamore Avenue). During the same year, it was decided to replace the old inn with a new building on a site just a few yards south of the original pub, on the corner of Hill Heads Road and Kingsley Avenue. The new Railway Inn was built adjacent to the extended sidings and coal depots associated

*The Railway Inn as it was in 1982.*

with Monkseaton Station close to the original waggonway crossing. All of these sidings were subsequently replaced with caravan storage/sales and a garage, and eventually the land was developed to incorporate a large supermarket and car park. Closely modelled on the nearby Quarry Inn which was also built in 1927, the Railway Inn underwent a full refurbishment in 2006, and despite an unflattering name change to Last Orders, the pub is still referred to by many of the locals as 'The Railway'.

# THE SEVEN STARS

## To be FOUGHT,

*At Mr. Taylor's Pit, at the Seven Stars, in Monk-Seaton.*

A MAIN of COCKS, betwixt William Sotheron and Hugh Bethell efqrs. To fhew fixty-one Cocks on each Side, for TEN GUINEAS a Battle, and One Hundred the Main or odd Battle.

To weigh on Monday the 8th of March next, and fight the 10th, 11th, 12th, and 13th following.

Feeders, { Mr. HENRY SMITH, for Mr. Sotheron / Mr. RICHARD SCOTT, for Mr. Bethell

There will be a good Ordinary at the above houfe during the Fighting.

☞ Two other Mains will be fought betwixt the above Gentle men, one at North Shields, and the other at Shire Moor.

The Seven Stars was an old inn which stood on the south east corner of the Fold, Monkseaton, on what is now the corner of Front Street and Rosebery Terrace, close to the present Ship Inn. Little is known of this pub, which is believed to date from the 1600s, and the only known references relate to a large one-acre rear garden which was planted with choice fruit trees. A sale notice of 1814 advertised the premises to be let and a schedule indicates that there was an illuminated cellar cock-pit with glass lights behind. Cock-fighting was a popular pastime throughout the eighteenth and nineteenth centuries. It was often referred to as the 'Royal Sport' and had had a number of notable followers including the Duke of Cleveland and Earl of Northumberland.

Contests were advertised as 'Gentlemen's Subscription Mains' but the 'sport' was actually popular with all classes. Established rural cock-pits were often no more than an uncovered earthwork, they were generally located in or near to villages. The pits consisted of a central fighting platform, 2.5m or more in diameter, surrounded by a shallow ditch and external bank. During the contest low boards were put on the platform to contain the birds. Three classes of birds were normally used – 'Stags' which were under one year old, 'Cocks' which were older, and 'Blenkards' or one-eyed veterans. Birds who refused to fight were known as 'Fugies' or 'Hamies'. Cock-fighting became a well publicised and financially well-backed 'sport'. As well as the local venues, cock-fighting also took place at local race meetings, usually in the morning, followed by the horse racing in the afternoon. Events were advertised in the local press, such as the *Newcastle Courant*. Prizes were normally in the region of 10-20 Guineas, however there were occasions when they could be as much as 500 Guineas. Sometimes the prizes for cock-fighting were of greater value than the awards for the local horse races. By the early nineteenth century opposition against the barbarity of cock-fighting was increasing, due to improved education and a religious revival which exerted moral pressures on society. Many of the local gentry turned to other pastimes, such as fox hunting, which at the time was more politically and socially acceptable. As many newspapers of the day carried announcements of such events, it could certainly be inferred that perhaps the villagers of Monkseaton took pleasure in witnessing the brutal mains involving these Cocks, Stags and Blenkards.

*The Seven Stars Inn was demolished soon after 1814, and replaced by two large stone built houses; 'Murie House' and 'Jessamine House' shown on the right of this picture. The white cottages beyond are part of the Fold. This area is now occupied by Rosebery Court sheltered housing.*

# THE SHIELING

As development of Beaumont Park and Red House Farm housing estates progressed during the 1980s and 1990s, a small area was laid out at the end of Hepscott Drive to accommodate a compact shopping and community area which also included proposals for a new public house. First built and opened in 1987 as 'The Shieling', the premises were based on a modern octagonal design derived from a 'Shieling' which is a small round hut or shelter – a structure which was once common in Scotland and Northern England as a place of refuge for shepherds tending their livestock. The name may also

have been applied to reflect the large expanse of farmland and fields which once stood in this area. In November 2004, after some alteration and refurbishment work had been carried out, the pub took a change of name to The 'Red House Farm', in keeping with the nearby area of housing by the same name.

# THE SHIP INN

The Ship Inn was originally built as a farmhouse and part of North West Farm in 1688 by a Thomas Mills, for the prominent Mills family of Monkseaton. The building stood slightly to the east of the present Ship Inn, on the site of what is now the junction of Percy Terrace and Lyndhurst Road. A fireplace, carved with the date 1688 stood in one of the upper rooms of the building, and above the fireplace, in Stucco, the coat of arms

*The fireplace in the original Ship Inn.*

of Charles II, with the Royal monogram: CR, was evident, along with the Stuart motto: 'Beati Pacifici', which means *'Blessed are the Peacemakers'*. The coat of arms formed the centre of a moulded frieze and just prior to demolition of the old Ship in 1923, it was removed by several public spirited local citizens, and given to Whitley Urban District Council, where it was preserved in the council chambers at Whitley Bay. The frieze has long since disappeared, however it is believed that the plaque eventually found its way to the Robin Hood Inn at Murton Village, where it now forms part of an architectural feature on a fireplace wall. It is likely that the farmhouse was converted to become an ale parlour in the late 1700s as the existence of some old documents dated 30th January 1790, announced the sale of some local property to be held at *'The house of William Winter at the Ship'*. Subsequent records dated 1801 show that the Ship Inn was in the possession of a Rev Edward Parker, who sold the premises that year to a George Duxfield, the son of Joseph Duxfield, of Red House Farm, who was still recorded as the landlord in 1841. The inn passed by inheritance to a Mrs Ann Arthur who is recorded as licensee between 1851 and 1855. Subsequent owners and licensees are: 1855; John Nicholson, 1873; Joseph Blake, 1876-1887; Thomas Arkley, 1893; Mrs Nicholson (widow of John Nicholson who ran the pub in 1855), 1897; Joseph Potts, 1910; Elizabeth Robinson.

In 1922, the Old Ship Inn was demolished, and in 1923, at a cost of £5,100 it was replaced with the present building, which was commissioned by the Northumberland Brewery Co. Ltd. (the then owners of Monkseaton Brewery), and was constructed just a few yards to the west, adjoining Rosebery Terrace. A carved stone plaque above the canopy and door reads: *"1688 – Ye Olde Ship Inn. Rebuilt 1923"*.

A conveyance dated 15th December 1934, shows that the building was sold to the Newcastle Breweries Ltd for the sum of £24,500. From its construction until the late 1970s the Ship Inn was internally, largely untouched and unaltered. As a building, the Ship had a lot of local charm, with many faithful customers who were characters in their own right too. It has always been very much a traditional local pub. On entering the main front door, a corridor led towards the back of the pub. The first door on the left ran into a small bar, which for many years was men only, and was frequented by a hard core of domino players. Off the corridor to the right, was a Select Room, which was also 'Gentlemen Only'. Drinks were served after ringing

*The original Ship Inn depicted in 1912. Scott & Robsons grocery shop and the old Black Horse Inn are visible to the right.*

a bell, and waiting for a member of staff to come and take your order and return to the table with the drinks. At the end of this corridor, a small lobby led to the toilets with another corridor to the left, which linked with the lounge bar, which was also served by a member of staff taking orders at the tables. A small sitting room also ran off to the right. Back outside, the corner door led into a small off sales shop, and a door at the side led directly into the lounge bar. When the pub underwent alterations during the 1970s, this door was bricked up, and replaced with a window. The window of the off

sales shop was also removed and replaced with two smaller windows to match the rest of the frontage, and apart from minor cosmetic changes, are the only external features which have changed since the Ship was built. Internally, the main corridor disappeared, and along with the select room became an extension of the bar. The small sitting room became the ladies toilets, and the off sales shop was altered to combine with the lounge bar, and renamed: 'The Captain's Cabin'. The manager's residence is situated on the upper first floor,

*The New Ship Inn under construction in 1922.*

accessed by a door and stairway at the rear of the pub, and although unconfirmed, it is understood that part of the first floor was once dedicated to a public function or billiard room. Perhaps some of the best known and longest serving managers since the 1960s were; Stan Graham, Percy and Moira Young, Joyce Eaton-Hall and Fred Turnbull, a former professional football player who played as a defender for Aston Villa between 1966 and 1974 until injury forced his retirement.

The following colourfully worded extract was taken from the *Shields Daily News*, dated Monday 2nd October 1865:

## Assault at Monkseaton

Thomas Nicholson, farmer, Whitley, was summoned for having assaulted Joseph Dunn, butcher, Monkseaton. Mr Kewney appeared, for complainant, who said that on the 22nd ult. He was in the Ship Inn Public House, Monkseaton, the defendant being here at the same time. While drinking a glass of ale, defendant offered to make a bet with complainant that he dare not take his (defendant's) cap off his head, for if he did so, his dog would seize him (complainant). Dunn declined making any such bet, but after being importuned by Nicholson he took his (Nicholson's) cap off – the dog not touching him. Upon this, Nicholson who was lying in a recumbent position upon a long settle, rose up and struck Dunn and knocked him down. While down, Nicholson continued to strike Dunn, until he was almost insensible. Defendant said complainant had given the first provocation. The bench fined Nicholson 5s and costs.

*The Ship Inn, soon after completion of building work in 1923.*

# MEMORIES OF THE SHIP INN

The following edited extract, written by a contributor to North Shields Library Club recalls some personal memories and recollections which typifies the Ship Inn during the 1970s:

'I remember many good times in Monkseaton pubs. I became 18 (and thus able to drink legally) in 1974. The Ship in Monkseaton was my main haunt. When I first started using the pub, it had 4 bars. The public bar was men only and revolved around dominoes. It was only a small bar, and the three tables therein were permanently occupied during evening sessions with domino players, and even on weekday lunchtimes, there was always one table with five players busily engaged in dominoes. The rules were strict. One did not leave the table whilst a hand was in progress. If you had to go to the loo, you asked an onlooker to play your hand, in order that the game was not interrupted. The game played was exclusively 'Thirty-ones', in which you played your hand and, at its end, the number of spots on your remaining dominoes were noted down. Hands were played successively, and when your cumulative score exceeded 30, you were out. It was 5p per game with 1p per knock, but remembering that Exhibition Ale was 16p per pint, the cumulative pot was quite substantial if you were lucky enough to win it. The public bar also had two little tables that were used by non-domino players.

The pub had many characters. The landlord, Percy Young, was very keen on bowls and was a member of Souter Park Bowls Club. A very smartly dressed man, Percy was a strict landlord, but if you got a bit drunk in the public bar, he would simply refuse to sell you any more beer, and would tell you to go home and come back tomorrow. He knew his customers, and their alcoholic capacities, extremely well, and remains one of my heroes to this day. Other characters included Wally, a lobster fisherman. He hated people who left ready-made cigarettes burning in the ashtray, and would sometimes extinguish them with his beer. Alec was a dapper man in his fifties, when I knew him. Ex-army, he would always insist that dominoes were laid on the table in a 'straight, regimental' fashion. We had two Sid's. One was diabetic and seldom drank alcohol; the other was an ex-policeman who gave me a lot of good advice and guidance in my early maturity. All were keen domino players. The bulk of the public bar customers were working-class men, but the tendency was for such men to dress smartly – suit, shirt and tie, when they came out for an evening's drinking. Ken, who was a bit of an intellectual, would come into the bar dressed in slacks, jacket and open-necked shirt. His dad, who was a regular, was deaf, and Ken would converse with him using sign language.

The public bar furnishings were basic. Benches, padded and finished in Rexine, lined the walls, and a few wooden stools with similar coverings, provided the remaining seating. Three rectangular wooden tables topped with Melamine and permanently occupied with domino boards, were in evidence, and two little round tables occupied the remaining space. King Arthur and his Knights were not in evidence. The serving bar could accommodate perhaps ten standing drinkers. Beers dispensed were Newcastle IPA, Exhibition and Harp Lager, through electric pumps. Draught Guinness was also available on pump. Bottled beers were Newcastle Brown and Amber; Jubilee Stout, McEwen's strong ale and Holsten Pils lager. Bottled Guinness, by the half or pint, also lurked behind the

bar. The main tobacco dispensary was also in the public bar. Embassy Regal, Capstan Full Strength and Woodbines were the main trade. You could also get Kensitas, Players and Golden Virginia, along with St Bruno, Capstan, Condor, Erinmore and a few plug pipe tobaccos.

From the public bar, one progressed to the select room. This was 'Gentlemen Only' and a tie was de riguer. The Monkseaton Moot met therein. This was a gathering of savants who met regularly and hired in speakers who addressed the august assembly on subjects of interest. I did not make much use of this facility, being young and daft in those days. The room was pushily furnished. It had no serving bar, drinks being obtained by pushing a bell push on the wall. A member of the bar staff would appear, take your order, and return with your drinks upon a tray.

Between the public and select, there was a lobby in which reposed a fruit machine. A few worthies would congregate there, placing their drinks on the solitary table, and observing or playing the machine; whilst diverting themselves by watching those who visited the Gents, entrance to which was adjacent to this nondescript

*The Ship Lounge in 2003.*

arena. A corridor linked this lobby to the lounge bar, but, abutting directly on to this passage was the sitting room. This room was furnished in the same style as the public bar, but admitted women, and had a television set. Lunchtimes found the room occupied by horse-racing devotees, nipping in and out to Fred Laidlaw's betting shop, or to the other Turf Accountant's premises, the name of which escapes me. Evenings saw working-class couples enjoying the basic ambience of the room. There was no serving bar in the sitting room. A bell summoned the bar staff who would dispense ale and Jubilee Stout etc from a tray to the seated imbibers.

The lounge was the plus ultra of the establishment. Presided over by Moira, Percy Young's stalwart wife, this magnificent room was furnished in opulent green leather, with heavy tables of cast iron topped with a gold-coloured metal. Boots could be lost in the pile of the carpet. Strangely enough, this Ultima Thule housed a mixture of the suited and booted, along with some of the scruffiest individuals one could find. In some circles, in the early to mid 1970s, long hair and elbow-patches were marks of respect and signatures of brain and intellect. This room was dubbed 'The Captain's Cabin' by the owning brewery.

The Ship sold no food, except for crisps etc. A few experiments were made with the sale of hot dogs and toasted sandwiches, but in the final analysis, the pub was a very traditional local.

Since I left Monkseaton in 1976 in search of work, the Ship still remains in my mind and memory, and I dedicate this little missive to the memory of those who drank in The Ship and have passed on, and to Percy and Moira Young in particular.'

# THE THREE HORSE SHOES INN / ROSE COTTAGE

Rose Cottage was situated on the west side of Chapel Lane and stood slightly to the north of the actual Chapel, separated only by a small blacksmiths shop which stood between the two buildings. It is recorded that the Inn dates from 1795 when it opened as an ale house under the name of The Three Horse Shoes.

Although there is no definitive evidence, an interesting tale exists that in the late 1700s, an old sea captain and his crew were shipwrecked on Whitley Beach during this year, and travelled to Monkseaton where they discovered a band of smugglers living in Rose Cottage. The captain is said to have ousted the smugglers and made his home in the cottage, where he started to brew ale which he sold to locals and passing travellers. As a result, the captain then opened up the house as an inn shortly afterwards and named it as The Three Horse Shoes. It is however interesting to note that in 1799, the innkeeper at the Three Horse Shoes is recorded as a Robert Mills, who was an old Greenland Whaler, so the likelihood is that the tale may have been a fanciful exaggeration of the truth.

On 24th April 1799, the Tynemouth Association for the Prosecution of Felons offered a reward of two Guineas to anyone who could offer any

*The Three Horse Shoes Inn c.1900.*

information leading to the conviction of thieves who had stolen poultry from Robert Mills at the Three Horse Shoes Inn.

In 1827, the proprietor of the inn was still recorded as Robert Mills, which in 1841, had changed to a John Lowery, and in 1845 to a Margaret or 'Peggy' Lowery.

It would appear that Robert Davidson* took ownership around 1862, as he was responsible for a partial rebuild of the premises. It is unclear when the inn actually closed but afterwards, it became a shop, a post office and latterly a private residence.

The property underwent an extensive rebuild in the early 1930s to become a private detached residence, and in later years was locally referred to and nicknamed 'Garnicks Cottage', so named after Alec Garnick, a builder who was the last resident.

The house, which stood on the corner of Chapel Lane next to the back lane of Front Street fell into a state of disrepair and was demolished in 1998 to be replaced by a new detached building, which is used as a small residential centre for people with learning disabilities.

* Robert Davidson will be featured in **Monkseaton Village Volume Two**.

# BIOGRAPHY – CHARLIE STEEL

Charlie Steel was born in Newcastle upon Tyne, and was a former pupil of Langley Avenue and Monkseaton County Secondary Schools. On leaving, he spent eight years in the printing trade as a Graphic Artist and Photographer and in 1975 he joined Northumbria Police where he served for 30 years until his retirement in 2005.

Charlie has a passionate interest in the local history of the North Tyneside area, particularly Monkseaton and Whitley Bay, where he has lived for most of his life.

Charlie's Great Grandfather; George Steel, was a prominent businessman in Whitley Village at the turn of the century, and founded Steels Nursery Gardens which were situated on Whitley Road (now Park View) opposite St Paul's Church, occupying the area of land between what is now the Fat Ox and Norham Road, to the back of Roxburgh Terrace, including the site of the former bus station, where the shops and new shopping Mall are now situated. George Steel also owned land at West Park, Hill Heads, the site of the present Ice Rink and Cricket Field. (Much of the Steel family history is featured in a book entitled; *Whitley Bay*, by John Alexander, published by Sutton Publishing in 2000).

Over the years, Charlie has written many local history articles for several regional publications which include *The Northumbrian, Roundabout Monkseaton* and *Roundabout Tynemouth* and the North Shields Directory

Having a particular fascination with the history of Monkseaton and Whitley Bay, he compiled a book entitled *Monkseaton & Hillheads*, which was first published in 2000,

www.monkseaton.info

and this was expanded in 2008 with his website: www.monkseaton.info which is dedicated to the history of Monkseaton. The masthead for the website is taken from a painting by Edith F. Grey, an artist who lived in Monkseaton for a number of years, and illustrates a view of the village looking west on Front Street during the early 1800s when access to the main street was through a set of farm gates.

In this book and on his website, Charlie has attempted to trigger a sense of nostalgia for those people who may remember Monkseaton as it was, and for those who have an interest in our local heritage; it will hopefully illustrate a different perspective of what used to be.

As urban development continually progresses, small elements of our past history are gradually eroded, and begin to slip away. This is Charlie's contribution – sharing the past in words and pictures.